Mindshifts

Parts

Introduction

"Mom asks "What did you learn?". He answers,

"Nothing".

It was a cold, rousing December morning.
Mason got up from his bed at a sharp 6:15 in the
morning. He's the typical 14-year-old you'd come
across every day. The typical 14-year-old who dashed
across his kitchen floor, gulping cereal down his throat
as he ran towards the bus already running through its
street. He goes to class, and 20 minutes into his first
hour, Algebra I class, he's dozed off. 20 minutes into his
second hour, he's doing homework for another class. 20
minutes into his third, and his phone is prompted up

on his knee below the desk. He's on YouTube, watching a video about the antics of Lyndon Baynes Johnson, unknown to his Physics teacher. He eats lunch. Fourth hour, he's taking down notes and looking at the clock. Fifth hour? He's daydreaming about all the TV he's about to watch when he comes back. Sixth hour, he answers questions regarding his short-term memory of Spanish vocabulary. The moment it's done, so is the last time he plans to ever write those words again.

He comes back home. Mom asks, "What did you learn?". He answers, "Nothing". The pattern goes on for 4 more years. He goes to college. Gets a job and adds to the workforce.

The twist? His job wasn't at all related to what he majored in. His previous job didn't even require a degree. He's part of a much larger phenomenon-underemployment, which stands at a rate of 13.7 percent, according to Investopedia. To add a push to the shove, nearly 80% of college graduates do not work in a field related to their major.

Mason isn't a real person. But he's part of a phenomena where many people are living the same life as Mason are- and the proposed solution to the root of the problem is allowing the degrees people hold to have meaning again. To get people what they pay for. The answer speaks a language of sweeping reform, but not of the right reform. This book that I'm writing to you-Mindshifts, thinks about the approach to reform differently- specifically, education reform.

In this book, you'll see three rebukes to the traditional languages of reform:

❖ **The world of education isn't changing. It's stagnant and needs to get with the times.** The truth is that the world of education is changing. Rapidly changing, and it's using the steadfast of technology to do so. What isn't happening is adaptive, public implementation that answers the call of a change in access to information.

❖ **The education system is a failure.** It's not. It was designed after the becoming of an economic workforce that needed a system that could quickly filter, rank and teach students based on the foundations of what they know, and to be able to reflect on what they know easily, consistently, and repeatedly.

❖ **Big solutions are the way you solve the qualms of education.** You don't need to upheave things from the ground up to improve public education. In many cases, such as high school curriculums, can find solutions from the top down, such as changing the priorities of college admissions.

To make this case, there's going to be some stories. Stories like the Lambda School, a variation of a trade school that saw its success, not by becoming a competitor to colleges, but through the small detail of clarifying what it intended to do: Teaching students how to code, and to get them career success by doing so.

The lessons extracted from Lambda, and stories like it, can help better paint the more realistic picture of education reform that I aim to highlight in this book. On a major note, it comes with the aforementioned problem- that the standard for educational success does not directly coordinate with jobs students are getting. While student debt has risen to a whopping 1.9 trillion, only 27% of students are getting a job in their major. The commonly proposed approach to solving this is by finding out how to make colleges better.

The thing is, that's not the particular solution at all. The problem isn't with colleges, it's with the degree, and what its utilities are in today's day and age. More than anything, a degree is a *signal* (a tool of predicting one's value in the workforce), for employers to use to hire new people into the economy, and, as you'll read later on, its predictive measurements have lost ground in their competitive utility, along with how accurate it is in presenting the data of newer attributes that the job market is asking for- attributes the degree was not meant to present during its inception. Of course, this solution isn't found by simply changing the system, but by making the right changes. By thinking small first, not big.

For those familiar in the startup scene, this is the textbook style of thinking in Eric Reiss' hit book, "The Lean Startup", which teaches the successes of "lean thinking", essentially being, to find a targeted problem, explore who that problem affects and how, and to use that data to form and execute a simple solution. Then, as the solution gets developed, it gets tested- made to fail, until the feedback loop is strong enough to integrate, iterate, and iterate into a success. It's the story of 'Burbn", a startup whose pitch was essentially that of Foursquare, with photos. Once it found out that there wasn't a simple forum to share photos, it pivoted and eventually formed into a startup that would eventually be bought out by Facebook (which had a similar story), for $1B. It's now better known as Instagram.

Lean thinking, however, isn't just for startups. It's a strategy for solving problems as a whole, a strategy I call Mindshifting- the idea of changing the perspective of how reform can be developed. In other words, it's Lean Thinking, but for political reform, rather than the startup.

The core of Lean Thinking is the concept of First Principles- a mindset construction by Elon Musk, and is defined by "a basic assumption that cannot be deduced any further", and at its core lies in scientific thinking, to certify what is absolute, and to doubt what is not certain. The system on its own is the core process that lies in finding the problem: *What is the core root of the problem occurring? What is the depth of that problem? What is the way that problem can be solved?

Lean thinking has found a notable level of success in startups- used in the strategies of startup development with incubators such as Y-Combinator, and has expanded well into the research sector, as Steve Blank states in his article "Why the Lean Startup Changes Everything", where he states, "In 2011 the U.S. National Science Foundation began using lean methods to commercialize basic science research in a program called the Innovation Corps. Eleven universities now teach the methods to hundreds of teams of senior research scientists across the United States". When it comes to creating a successful political approach to reform-education reform, this is the thinking style that both has shown, and has the capacity to be the template towards realigning the woes education does in fact face, of today, tomorrow, and the days after- to the economy of today, tomorrow, and the days after.

I've had my grasps with education- it's what I've written most consistently about in the past five years, initially speaking the language of reform I'm speaking against in this book, and that's precisely why writing this book has been as interesting for me as it hopefully will be for you to read. Five years ago, I wouldn't imagine making any shred of a case for changing education less than anything sounding of large, reformist methodology- but after spending a part of those five years learning more about the language of lean startups and finding the similarities they can pose with the fruits of policymaking, I saw an opening that wasn't discussed in the debates of education: lean thinking as a way to approach reform. Now, I'm not a professor. I haven't taught a single class, not a day in my life. I'm a student, and this the first book I've ever written. In any case, I shouldn't be the one writing about education- but nobody else is talking about this, so I'll be the first. Someone has to be.

This book is for anyone looking for a new way. For the political enthusiast- Mindshifts is a new way you can survey how bureaucratic reform can find a greater footing towards success, and how they can become successful. For the educators- and future educators, Mindshifts is a way to look at how to see education change, how to perceive it, and how you can try to see this form of reform happen around you locally. For the reader looking to see if there's a lesson they can fit into their own life- Mindshifts is a way to understand the thinking that have brought startups and solutions to success- an approach you yourself can implement in your own life. Lean thinking is not exclusive to anything- just to the limits of where you put it.

We're going to be exploring this in 3 different sections: Exploring the economic gap of education (Chapters 1-4), the private approach to the problems that make them up (Chapters 8-10), and two policy solutions that showcase two different approaches to how they solve problems (10-12).

The necessity of change has always been a conversation in the political sphere, but Mindshifts is a book about how that change happens, effectively. Mindshifts explores the level past that- how to change the way change is made, and how to change the way we change minds.

I am Macintosh.

"It gave voices to leaders who, otherwise, didn't have a shot in the dark to make themselves heard."

"Hello, I am Macintosh. It sure is nice to get out of that box."

Those were the first words the computer with the silly face spoke to an audience that had fallen in awe with Apple's 1984 Superbowl ad. The monumental desktop computer came stock with what was known as a G.U.I., or a graphic user interface, a concept stolen by Apple during a visit to Xerox Park back in the day. The idea was that, instead of writing commands as you would in your computer's command prompt to get something done, you would have this little gadget in the palm of your hand—a mouse. All you do is point and click at a visual image or button, and the computer would do it for you.

Of course, computers weren't always like this. That same 1984 ad that had grasped its pivotal moment in history was an ad that intended to mark an entirely new area in computing. As a woman's hurtling ax tore past a screen bearing a face characterized as "Big Brother," the closing text heroically proclaimed, "On January 24th, Apple Computer will introduce Macintosh. And you'll see why 1984 won't be like '1984.'"

The Macintosh wasn't simply a new P.C.; it was as the hero- whose outline was drawn onto the woman's shirt flinging the computer. The George Orwell to then computing giant's I.B.M. Big Brother.

Before the G.U.I., there was Microsoft D.O.S., the
operating system that would be running the I.B.M.
Model 5150; a P.C. released three years before the
Macintosh. According to the NYT, in 1983, "Analysts
estimate that I.B.M. sold 175,000 to 200,000
computers in 1982, its first full year on the market, and
will sell at least 400,000 to 500,000 this year". Section 3,
Page 1.

I.B.M. was a superpower, the dominating leader in
mainframe computing. Like D.O.S. before the G.U.I.,
there was Mainframe Computing before the P.C.,
which looked like a modem on steroids. Mainframes
would mask walls around enterprises all over. They
didn't look anything like the modern computer today
and initially would be used by punching in commands
and getting the result printed out. There weren't any

screens- one couldn't see what they were programming, let alone interacting with the interface with a mouse.

Eventually came the Xerox Alto, a computer with a monitor- or a screen that could allow users to see what they had been typing down in the first place. While its screen changed, how to use it didn't.

Until the release of Macintosh, all interaction towards a computer was text-based programming, interacting like traditional programming languages, like Java. It had to be layer atop an operating system, which is the primary software and automatic commands a computing system uses to operate- operating systems like Microsoft D.O.S., which worked not-to-differently from the command prompt seen on Windows Computers today. To run a computer in 1981, you'd need to be familiar with at least amateur-level coding.

On a more macro level, that meant that the power of a computer wasn't accessible by everyone- only a select few. Information and automation still were not at a level of easy access- but that all changed with the G.U.I. It was visual, simple, and straightforward. It was the technological equivalent of "Explain it to me like I'm 6." It was as simple as pointing and clicking.

It worked the way that our minds work, and it made computing, and the extensions of power it could give to one's brain, more accessible and easier than ever. It also was a pivotal moment in which our economies of scale would quickly begin to change. Inevitably, Microsoft followed suit, and it did it for computers that business owners could thrive on. Affordable, rich with stock software, and customization, the G.U.I. would take the workforce by storm. It was also the pivotal moment in which the capacity to produce would begin skyrocketing, with software and service coming after one another, creating a boom in productive utilities unheard of in history. It made billionaires. It formed stock bubbles that would be famed in the glory of the past. It gave voices to leaders who otherwise didn't have a shot in the dark to make themselves heard.

That G.U.I. was a pivotal moment in forming an economy and an economy that had already matured out of valuing labor into one that would value skills and trade. The computer created a world at its most competitive- it had to do with the formation of a knowledge economy or an economy that trades on what you know as the main centerpiece of value. If you knew how computers work, you had a great gig to settle on out of school. If you knew how to get people to click on links, you were the star of the ad agency. If you knew different languages, writing skills, political theories, or, about anything, you would very likely find it much easier to find a demand for it. Once that happens, you need more people who know more things. Intellectual capital gets mined like Californian gold.

Eventually, you have an economy, designed from the ground up, to be trading knowledge like commodities by placing value and trades based on what you have stored in your head. More specifically, Greene College Professor Tevjan Pettingger articulates it as "The sector of the economy which is increasingly based on knowledge-intensive activities, creating a greater reliance on intellectual capital rather than physical inputs."

The problem, with these economies, would be the fundamental nature of advantage, which differs from the general benefits of production, as described by

Robert Unger's *The Knowledge Economy*, in which

Unger states:

As new wealth gets accumulated in the knowledge

economy, the distance separating this economy from

the vast periphery of production generates inequalities

that the traditional devices for attenuating inequality

are inadequate to master. These devices protect

conventional small businesses and compensate

redistribution by tax and transfer: progressive taxation

and redistributive social spending. They generate a

secondary distribution of economic advantage by

contrast to the arrangements shaping the primary

distribution. (Unger, 2017)

The most notable point to mention here isn't that

knowledge was nonexistent within economies before it.

Work that was more intellectually intensive drove the production process, but it was not active within it. Think, the difference between the construction of theorizing an assembly line at Ford versus working at the assembly line at Ford. Two very different constructions with very different demands.

This change in knowledge is where the fundamentals of education come in, more specifically, higher education, which was highly exclusive at first. In the paper, "The Shaping of Higher Education: The Formative Years in the United States, 1890 to 1940." by Claudia Goldin and Lawrence F. Katz describes "The business of colleges and universities in the creation and diffusion of knowledge." In essence, facts were like spending money. (Goldin, Katz, 1999)

Columbia is a great case. Its inception is described as where "Samuel Johnson held the first classes in a new schoolhouse adjoining Trinity Church, located on what is now lower Broadway in Manhattan. There were eight students in the class. At King's College, the future leaders of colonial society could receive an education designed to "enlarge the Mind, improve the Understanding, polish the whole Man, and qualify them to support the brightest Characters in all the elevated stations in life." (Columbia)

The exclusive model worked with an earlier economy, but as times changed, so would schools. A notable one would be the inception of Michigan State University, the first land-grant university built in the United States of America, resemblance of a public college that would grow student access to education as people started the initial transition towards industrialization in America,

courtesy of the Morril Act of 1862, which was "An Act
Donating public lands to the several States and
[Territories] which may provide colleges for the benefit
of agriculture and the Mechanic arts." (Morril Act,
1862)

The example this points to is explicitly the adaptation
of education to the economy. As time went by, so did
the expansion of majors, students, student
requirements, and the purpose. What were once
institutions of higher learning would change
dramatically in their styles, such as grading, which was
secret during the creation of a 0-4 scale at Yale
University. Things like behavior and participation held
higher significance. Now, back in the infancy of early
education, the point wasn't to compete- because if you
were in university, you already had what virtually
nobody else did: a degree. A nominal signature of

wisdom, handed by world-class chefs of bundled information, served to you on a silver plate. Move to the 1940s, and you have an A-F, standard 100-point system sweeping through schools and piles of admissions papers. 1943 was the year that the S.A.T. became a test of merit.

A degree was no longer the ivory pedigree. It was the honor of being the best of the best; if you were an apple in the best tree, that was great. But come from a prestigious school with straight A's and a 99 percentile S.A.T. score, and you're not just an apple. You're an apple that's boiled, on a stick, and covered in caramel.

It's important to note that at the time, we were going through a war. Not just any conflict, but world War II, a fight embedded in history as one drowned in battles of justice, around the same time as the advent of the nuclear bomb. This economy wasn't any economy; it was a war economy. We needed people to produce quickly and in droves. Our minds required working at the forefront of labs, people scouting intelligence. We needed people who could sell bonds, tell the world what was happening around us. We needed memory in the minds of our youth. We needed them to read, write, do complex math, and understand science because the more well-rounded we were, the more we could fight this war. And thus came the advent of an education system that could produce minds that could follow the rules quickly and efficiently to know what the world couldn't and do without causing disruption.

Later, that thinking style was perfect for businesses to use, especially during an economic upturn where taxes were sliced open. A conservative revolution meant companies would have to compete more and more intensely, with the advent of the Swiss Army Knives of productivity on everyone's hands.

The growth of a minimum wage, booming business, and a world of more production meant merit was the north star for the economy. Saying that you knew things better than others, who already knew it, better than others, that was the infrastructure work needed to justify the wages its employees got. In the world of picket fences, two kids, and a car, money was the quintessential object of affection.

Our system obliged. And from there, we would begin to see the government utilize education as a predictive asset rather than a fundamental one. When everything began to change, this system could be immortal in a world of crystallized knowledge. The problem was, we couldn't predict how knowledge would become so radically decentralized in the 21st century, where a search bar could become a Pandora's Box for the world's secrets. And so, comes the gap that education would form with technology and a relationship that would have to struggle with strain and stardom.

In Summary:

- The context of an economy with new demands comes from the dawn of modern-day computing. Before modern-day computing, the ability to operate and easily access information was concentrated in the power of a select few, taking an extensive number of resources and skills to do so. It wasn't until the creation of a G.U.I. (Point-and Click), in which computing became accessible.

- When computing did become truly mainstream, it accelerated an economy already moving away from traditional labor to one that deeply necessitated mental knowledge and skills as the standard for conventional jobs. If somebody knew something, they could monetize it somehow, shape or form, breeding a

"Knowledge Economy," or an economy prioritizing what one knows over what they are physically capable of doing.

- From the initial period of 1890-1940, the primary purpose of colleges was to create a leg-up by sharing knowledge that was exclusive to the students it had, giving them a significant leg-up in the workforce where access to knowledge wasn't open. It was a system designed to be highly exclusive and not part of a traditional education system to obtain a job.

- As the economy changed, however, so did the demand for higher education, and as a result, more land was given for universities to expand or open. Majors and trades were now no longer bearing the purpose it had been designed for, quickly transforming into a mainstream part of the education timeline of a student.

- Because of this change, so did the learning mechanisms, which needed to focus more on quickly discerning students en masse from each other, with more levels of data in assistance for it. Getting a degree was no longer discernible enough- which prompted the initial creation of the grading system used today.

- The shape of education, as a result, would change. Instead of being a form of enrichment used in competition, it would become a predictive system designed to place and organize groups into the system, which meant that it would have to stray from its initial roots that focused solely on enrichment to adapt.

It's the economy,

stupid.

"When you see a student come from an elite school, it's not about what they know; it's the fact that they got in."

How does a changing workforce change the value education provides?

Tailoring isn't exclusive to clothes- the gap mentioned previously was the effect of the initial success of an education system economically tailored like a bespoke, shawl lapel suit fresh from Savile's Row. Tying education to economics makes it seem pointless to change a system that prides itself on merit.

But change is a funny thing, and when it comes to production within an economy, technology catalyzes it. It enables people to not only expand their reach but expand how they can do so. This reach changes factors such as average working hours, job preparation demand, skills, and the growth of U.S wages. Then, the desire for what skills a student obtains during education also changes. If that doesn't happen- an **economic gap** occurs- where the students haven't learned what a changed economy wants. Still, they also make up a significant portion of the labor force, forming a growth in problems such as underemployment.

What does this look like, specifically?

According to the economic data survey, "The Decline of Working Hours per Year after the Industrial Revolution," by Michael Huberman and Chris Minns, the weekly work hours from 1950-2000 went from 42.40 hours a week to 40.25.

Pew Research Center's 2016 State of American Jobs also found "... that interpersonal skills, critical thinking, and good writing and communications skills are the most important skills for doing their jobs".

Jobs requiring above average preparation and training grew from 50-83% from 1980-2016, respectively, and finally, that "From 1990 to 2015, the average earnings in jobs more reliant on social or analytical skills have also increased more than the average earnings in jobs requiring more intensive physical skills.".

The primary components are that of the same working hours, a massive rise in the demand for intellectual skill, and that those very same jobs that have those demands have grown immensely. But while that standard grew, the skills needed changed to being more on the angle of quality production, emphasizing cooperative function and deep thinking over being put in line and being well-rounded in one's work. In an economy where specialization is easily accessible from a google search, the consequences of hiring employees that can be autonomous and work well in the company are significantly lower.

It's also the perfect cocktail for another type of economy- a 'gig' economy. Personal production from computing means that a job can be bought, essentially on demand. It's cutthroat competition in its rawest form. It comes down to who can perform a position best and how this person can signal that - because those same interpersonal skills aren't the foundational topics taught in universities. It's harder to win by signaling that you can know how to do it, easier if you can show you're the best at it.

Imagine, for a moment, if you will, that you're a graphic designer out of Boston. Rent is expensive, and every week, you need to find a way to keep making ends meet. But getting an industrial job in this industry isn't easy unless you're an executive designer- which you are not. Your alternative is to do a gig. To do that, you've got to show your value- what you've designed, what others feel about it, and most importantly, that you're the best option. You use a platform like Fiverr, which may keep things running back in your Boston apartment by the gig.

Gigs have already begun to seep through the cracks of the American Economy, noted specifically in **Rich Fitzgerald, Trevor Brown, and Molly Turner's paper, "The Future of Work,"** The piece states that **"The number of self-employed individuals soared by over 19 percent from 2005 to 2015", where certain counties, for example, see substantial levels of change in gig workers, such as Palm Beach County, FL, where non-employer establishments have grown by 43.2%. (R. Fitzgerald, T. Brown, M. Turner, "The Future of Work," 2017).**

This development in gigs is signaled in themselves, indicating what people need and the demands of work. The question is no longer whether someone can get into a line or how much they know. It's whether they can get the job done at the standard that they advertise themselves to be. Right now, degrees are signals more than anything else. When you see a student come from an elite school, it's not about what they know; it's the fact that they got in. In the past- before the age of the mainstream internet, a degree was a way to stand out. They indicated what a person specifically knew when they got to work and how exclusive their knowledge was. Back when the workforce did not have borderline unfiltered access to a decentralized human knowledge database, degrees meant that a person already had the tools in-store to outcompete another candidate. In today's day and age, though- that's changed. Now, a degree reflects how studious one is, how well they did in high school, what connections they likely made, and, most primarily, a source that produces a predictor to an employer as to how they will perform. It doesn't indicate that a person has all the tools in-store to outcompete another candidate like it once did.

But that also reveals another, more profound desire in the workforce.

It's the philosophy of "Show Me." That's a philosophy that doesn't necessarily mean a degree is crucial; it's a promise of good work. While it can be done, to some extent in the form of a degree- it doesn't show that work getting done. In contrast, a "Show Me" might mean a portfolio, an achievement, or a full-blown pitch. One the visualizes effort, diligence, and work quality in front of someone.

The world of public education lacks other forms of signaling- student's come out primarily with a degree. Like any gap one might see in economic needs, that can result in people trying to fix that gap themselves through private companies. One of them is Praxis, a new-age school that emphasizes self-learning and apprenticeships as the primary form of education, to the funnel of full-time work, in a world of gigs. 93% of its students receive full-time offers, with an average starting salary of $50K. Compared to the average bachelor's degree holder's salary of $50,600, with a 3.9% unemployment rate. The kicker, though, is the underemployment rate, which is a remarkable 33.8%. (Praxis, 2017)

Praxis doesn't have majors. In my interview with the founder of Praxis (as well as his LinkedIn competitor, Crash), Isaac Morehouse, that was made quite clear:

"What we're teaching you is stuff that I think is more fundamental, and that's mindsets that's the idea that I can learn anything if I'm curious if I'm motivated. Oh, I want to do this job, and this job requires me to know Final Cut Pro. Let me learn Final Cut Pro and a practice we've never wanted to try to be the best in the world at teaching any one specific skill. We want to be the best in the world at helping people realize that they can learn anything with the resources out there and create a mindset of self-ownership and self-discipline."

They specialize in mindset- the ability for students to be autonomous in learning. There aren't tests; there are projects. Students don't get unpaid internships; they take apprenticeships where they break even. Then the employer can decide whether that same student will work with them later and give them a full-time offer. There's no grade, and there's no GPA- it's signaling in its rawest form- providing value for free.

The power of "Show-Me" credentials goes further with pitch-based platforms like Crash, where, instead of listing a resume, people will 'pitch' to a handful of companies, showing them examples of tailored work, proving that they have what it takes to join the team. The logic behind the initial testing of this job-hunting style was explicit. The most formidable candidates had to pitch themselves by putting together projects, sending something tailored to that company, says "hey, here's who I am, here's what I made for you." In the words of the founder, "that's huge... it's a signal market."

Thereby comes the case that public education must battle- realigning itself with a new economy by reforming the way we grade and signal students, and potentially even rewiring the role of public education in a gig economy. This case is a battle plagued with lobbying and policies that leverage the system we have right now, and it has a lot to learn from the effectiveness of the private sector.

Summary:

- Economies' change and technological progress enable a workforce to adapt towards further productive reaches and the method in which it functions. As crews change, so make the demands expected of students, and as a result, the systems that build them.

- Today's education system works for a vastly different workforce, where simple knowledge made the differentiating process simple through degrees. They could quickly indicate specialty and elite training relative to the population.

- Today's economy has changed rapidly, primarily through the usage of contract work in contrast to employment. The demands of new students have also changed, with the most desired skills being how people work and how well they can do so- not what they know off the gate.

- The change in the economy comes from the internet, which decentralized access to knowledge that would otherwise be kept more exclusive.

- Degrees are an issue of specialization, but as they became more and more standard, what specialized a degree-holder became more specific. At the same time, degrees slowly began to evolve into predictors of performance as their primary utility. This process is also known as signaling and predicting how well a potential employee will do is a natural part of the hiring process.

- As time has gone by, those predictions demand to be more accurate, and options such as portfolios and pitches offer more visual,

product, and skin-in-the-game over a degree.
This change in demand resulted in an economic
gap- where the workforce is desiring a different
set of skills and signals from job prospects.
However, a significant share of students lacks
those assets coming out of college, creating
underemployment problems and jobs unrelated
to degree fields.

Beta Tests.

"The experiments being run are the bug-testers going

nuclear, trying to find out what goes where."

What are the effects of legislative lag in education? How does the lean thinking approach reduce them?

There's an observation that's to be made in the industry. Industries are like phone companies; when the product lags, bug-fixers become a team gone nuclear, scrambling to smooth whatever thing that's stopping the operating system on your phone from aggravating you any more than it already has. How well it works becomes a direct reflection of the quality and care somebody put into making sure that your phone feels more like a Swiss Army Knife than a razor blade scraping the bottom of your foot. In education, that's no different.

The lag stemming from education is like one of those bugs- but instead of it being on the phone, it's on paper. It's important to note the lag isn't the problem that educational bug-fixers are rushing to solve- it's what that lag *produces* that is the problem.

Retake the example of the phone- you don't become frustrated because your phone is frozen. You get frustrated because when you try to type a sentence, it takes a minute before you receive any feedback before you hit 'send.' If the phone was freezing up when you weren't using it, it doesn't pose much of a cost to you at all. Likewise, the presence of lag in reform isn't what creates frustration in education; it's the fact that reform is like one of the sentences being typed. The economy is the conversation. It's not 'sent' when it's needed, but after.

A great example of this comes from student loans, where the cost of college has risen dramatically, but wages have not. The change in what makes a good signal provokes a changed lust in employers worldwide with the rise of gigs and contracts. They are meant to answer the question of "who can get this done?" by getting it done before it's even asked.

The onslaught of imbalance towards the cost of a degree and the return on investment doesn't bode well in an economy that operates on credit, precisely because it takes a return on that investment to pay off that debt. With gigs enabling a more cutthroat workforce, passing through a set of hoops doesn't set one up to the top. It favors one person who prepares, performs, and charms better than anyone else- thus fewer people getting the return on investment needed to pay the debt.

The report from The Center for American Progress, "Addressing the $1.5 Trillion in Federal Student Loan Debt", by Ben Miller, Colleen Campbell, Brent Cohen, and Charlotte Hancock, has got a number.

It states, "About 43 million adult Americans—roughly one-sixth of the U.S. population older than age 18— currently carry a federal student loan and owe $1.5 trillion in federal student loan debt..."

That's 1/6th of the U.S population burdened in a loss of credit that affects the home they can buy, which affects the job they can get, the schools their children go to as well as what college can be afforded, what consumer goods can be bought, and the investments they can afford to make.

For incoming students, the discussion about financing college comes from Financial Aid, coming in the form of grants and scholarships to make college more affordable. This dual-working system was formed in 1965 through the formation of the FAFSA (Free Application for Federal Student Aid). The problem of college expense started to arise when it became a more popular option among the working class, with the cost of college inflating nearly 498.49% from 1982-2011, with about 12.25 million people enrolling in college in 1985, to 20.1 million people enrolling in 2011, a

64.0816% difference in per-year enrollment over 26 years. The CPI, in contrast, inflated 114.85% in the same time range. ("Inflation Data: Education Inflation," n.d.)

That cost of tuition marks a fitting example of substantive reform to change cost structure from a notably rapid influx of enrollment caused by the changes of economic demands arising from financial workers. The root of that comes from the rise of competitive colleges would provide a surge that didn't always exist. That's where the effects of lag begin to show: In the case of tuition, it's not been adapted to the way the workforce operates today, and students literally pay the price for it. Literally paying the price- that's the specific problem.

Legislation and reform take time. By reforming the laws regarding student loans, the rules regarding bankruptcy and student loan repayment would have to be considered and adopted. The legislative crisis that would have to be solved was how one would adequately put a price tag on education. That, in turn, forms another question- where the answer starts. That's the question of what public- and higher education's very identity. Is it a place primarily designed for the pursuit of knowledge? Or is it a place primarily intended for students to be funneled into work? Is it a public good, or does it best serve a specific type of student?

These questions can't simply be answered by one educator, an activist, or even the United States president. It's going lean- asking the **initial** question of what education's role is within a nation and asking what the part of knowledge is within an economy. It's asking what skills are a priority. It's asking the question of who should be getting the best shot at a better life. It asks what's fair and what isn't. That can't be answered simply through a governmental response. It takes experimenting. Running tests locally to see what works. It means working with the idea of knowing that we don't know what could come of the next generation that we did before. It takes the luxury of being willing and unable to understand what mistakes can't be repeated.

When it comes to solving the problems of lag, it means that it takes private sectors that can fail in front of millions without affecting the very soil that is the nation's youth. The experiments being run are the bug-testers going nuclear, trying to find out what goes where.

The private education sector comprises notably content-producing companies like Khan Academy, Wolfram-Alpha, Udemy, Lambda, AltSchool, MasterClass, etc., brimmed with guides towards reform.

These companies were not formed to substitute essential education. They try to solve specific flaws that they see within the system. Khan Academy, for example, found its footing, not simply inputting videos online but scaling more personalized learning models online. More formidably, this model can be seen in Khan's experience with gifted programs, where, for one hour a week, he would be allowed to dive as deep into a topic as he would desire.

"The first time I went, I thought it was the biggest racket. I walked up to Miss Rouselle's desk, and she asked, "What do you like to do?" I was like, I'm seven

years old—shouldn't you be telling me what to do? But

I said, "I like to draw. I like puzzles." She said, "OK,

have you used oil paints? Have you done Mind

Benders?" Soon I looked forward to that hour more

than I did to spending the night at my friend's house.

And I learned more that applies to what I do today

than in the five other hours of the day combined."

(Beard 2014)

The problem Khan Academy solved would come from

its depth- that learning didn't have to come from

others- but rather that curiosity, depth, and self-

proposed learning could be a powerful direction in

personalizing education- by letting students do it

themselves. The style of learning that Khan Academy

hones in on is assisting in autodidactic education. It

provides the content students need to know and guides

them through self-exploration. Students can test themselves on mastery, choose to dive deeper into a particular topic, and consistently use feedback to measure and attain confidence in whatever skill they are trying to build.

In contrast, this is much more difficult for students to obtain when they have to be graded, the curriculum has a vast set of goals to reach, and time is spent more on live instruction over content provision. That's not necessarily saying that Khan Academy is better- but rather that, for students that find themselves doing better when they explore on their own- it can be the antidote to their problem.

As previously mentioned, though, Khan Academy isn't the only company trying to change education. Different problems yield different solutions for other founders. That's where the beauty of reforming education in a world obsessed with the accuracy of a signal can be seen because there's certainly something to be said about the magic that comes from seeing kids getting things right- and seeing how that benefits everyone else in return. Now, we'll be revisiting Khan Academy in the coming chapters, but the point to be taken was **how** Khan Academy solved the problem, not just **what** problem it solved.

In Summary:

- To reiterate, the lag on its own isn't the problem- it's what the lag does.
- Student loans are a visible example of that problem- tuition has gone up dramatically while wages have not. This is in part, from a more

competitive market that gigs and contracts form.

- The problem of college expense started to arise when it became a more popular option among the working class, with the cost of college inflating nearly 498.49% from 1982-2011, with about 12.25 million people enrolling in college in 1985, to 20.1 million people enrolling in 2011, a 64.0816% difference in per-year enrollment over 26 years. The CPI, in contrast, inflated 114.85% in the same time range.

- That spike in student loans has drastic effects when more and more students can't pay them back- because the economy operates on credit, meaning that fewer houses, cars, and major purchases can be bought or leveraged by graduates at a notable scale. While tuition needs reform to adapt to the economy, it's not getting that change from a legislative standpoint.

- Tuition can't simply be solved by saying it must be absolved or changed entirely- there's a conversation it needs before that to find the correct answer. This is where lean thinking comes in- finding the fundamental problem: a lack of defining education- and knowledge's role in society today. Only then can you change the approach to tuition.

- This answer cannot be broadly brought up. It takes experimenting and 'bug-fixing. Private corporations, in this respect, can do that, while legislature does not, and the approach they take is an evident approach that can effectively find solutions to problems in education.

- An example of this is Khan Academy, which doesn't try to replace school but solve a **specific** problem. The problem Khan Academy solved came from depth- that learning didn't have to specifically come from another source- but rather that curiosity, depth, and self-proposed learning could be a powerful direction in personalizing education, letting students do it themselves.

Data and Greed.

"Just over one-half of all students with a score between 33 and 36 enrolled out of state, compared with only 12% of students with a score of 15 or lower."

How does the business of education work? How does that change the way effective reform can find its footing?

Like any functioning public agency, education, and specifically, higher education, is a sector not unfamiliar to the bouts of corporate-political ties. In specific, those ties hold the system together and are also the source of lagging the changes a system might need to adapt to ever-changing economies. Colleges and schools need to have money lining their pockets, or they can't function. People are not lining up to volunteer the teachings of complex thermonuclear physics- they trade their time for money. For such a vast system, money can be made in multiple different facets, all for other utilities.

It's also why education is not simply a topic left in the shadows. It's something put in the center, not the front. While not the star in presidential debates, teachers' unions brim with memberships and advocacy. The questions about the becoming of the next generation are always in question, the safety schools provide or the value they deliver in the workforce. Combine the political operations that it takes to push for the changes in a bureaucratic system, along with the flow of capital that makes its way along the hill, and you don't just have a system designed to teach students- but a system designed to formulate an industry all on its own. When that happens, public systems must move through not just the passing of bills to modify its capabilities but also consider and cooperate with the corporations behind education that also functions as an outlet to fund other political agendas that are far more front-facing voters.

Education isn't just a government sector. It's an industry. It's a business of trading knowledge, from how you gain it, to where, and to why. It's the bridge to the formation of a goal to achieve it, and bridges aren't built by just one manufacturer. Estimates conducted through the NeXt Knowledge Factbook in 2010, led by the Kellog School of Business, report the overall education industry in the U.S. to be worth nearly $1.3

Trillion, including Early Childhood Education, K-12, Higher Education, Adult Learning, Tutoring, Online Education, and Textbooks.

The basic foundations of the education industry, however, are rooted in higher education. Higher education is like a consumptive dictator on what products get to work in public education and what do not. Products like the SAT, tutorship, and textbooks find their life's work being enriched in the pool of college. The first thing to be looked at is the business specifically surrounding college applications to understand the education industry. They are a business within the company, reflecting how the industry operates, where the money comes from, and how it works.

 The admissions system- and the return it's designated to give, is a central driver in the business of education. As a result, it is also the corner-stoning diamond that every legislative action intended for K-College pathways depends on.

 The business of college admissions within the U.S. carries multiple hefty components: the portals for college applications, marketing within college applications, GPA data, testing scores data, student demographic data, student background data, recommendation letters, essays, all compiled into a form designed to predict whether a student will be a good fit within a university. **It all carries a central point of view: the provision of data.** In college admissions, data is the silver dollar within many coins that gives everything it's worth. People don't celebrate going into a school- they celebrate getting in. The reason is that their attendance is at the mercy of whether a university will take a chance on them based on what they see about them.

The beginnings of the admissions system come from marketing- what students the university wants applying. This goes about from reports primarily derived from standardized test makers, which report not only the overall test scores a student achieved but sectional scores as well. If a university wants the next class to show more mathematics skills, they can reach out to the students who scored a 780 on their SAT math section over the student that scored a 790 in reading. Multiple levels of filtering are what makes a class appear more decisive within a university.

But one's SAT score isn't the only thing a university will look towards when selecting students. For example, the CollegeBoard reports the SAT collecting information on students' ethnicity, gender, GPA, major, educational goals, financial aid plans, college preferences, ROTC plans, religion, high-school academics, athletics, and activities.

In Jeffery Silingo's article "How Colleges Use Big Data to Target, the Students They Want," Silingo mentions the work of Saint Louis University. In one case, he documented how Saint Louis University intended to find high-school students who stated they preferred to attend a private, religiously affiliated college; performed community service in high school. Due to the number of satisfied business majors on campus, they also wanted an entrepreneurial mindset (one of the questions asked of high-school students is whether they started a business or organization). "

That same year, the university was looking for students who wanted to expand its reach, which meant that it would also target students who showed a greater chance of coming out of state.

One of those predictors? The student ACT score, from which the ACT's E.M. Trends Report stated, "Just over one-half of all students with a score between 33 and 36 enrolled out of state, compared with only 12% of students with a score of 15 or lower."

Scores and demographics get colleges what they need-control over the diversity of the incoming class. This is a system where scores have decades worth of patterns to predict where students will go, plus data about who they are, where they are from, and what those students might be likely to do. The admissions system in the U.S. doesn't necessarily simply focus on the best students they can get; it's about the right student at the right time. The correct class means the right grants that could keep the lights running. A suitable course means the university can decide where it's headed without teaching a single student anything. The dictation over what a student body is made up of is powerful because, to the eyes of the education market, it gives the university a level of control over its brand that P.R. agents across the world would beg unto their knees to have.

Money is made on the test takings as well, with the SAT costing $49.50 per test without an essay and the ACT costing $46.00 per test. According to the Harland Clarke Holdings Corp, with those tests comes the student infamous Scantron, which made $119.9 million. Reports Full Year and Fourth Quarter 2012 Results.

The point being made here is that admissions data is not the only primary business that higher education yields and the method in which that data is collected and delivered. That data is also the root in which our education system funnels money through, specifically within K-12.

Within K-12 education, state governments will allocate an allowance produced on a per-student basis, combining contributions of both state and local payments that depend on the specific city questioned within the picture. City funding is wired mostly through the determination of property tax, where higher values on homes funds the schools, the residences will be sending their children to. This also means that areas of higher wealth can afford to spend more per student due to their ability to exceed the allowances needed. This means that students who are more likely to be well-fed, in a safer environment, with higher-paid staff, funding for testing are looped into communities where colleges, as well as the type of college- becomes a common recurrence. Students are then sent to more prestigious schools in higher percentages of the school body.

How does a school achieve that? Through displaying that its students have a better shot of making it into the right college, which can only be done by utilizing a standard levy, such as testing. Parents who are interested in moving to see that see where students with those scores might go and see if they can purchase a place that will send a child to that school. This, in turn, increases the demand for real estate in an area that becomes more and more desirable for families, growing school expenditure and turning it into a firm cycle. As a result, the schools that can test excellently- are the schools that build the neighborhoods around them. The data they send to universities isn't necessarily the best data representing a student- but it's the data the school and colleges both heavily desire to get work done.

The business of education and the admissions system that creates it is ingrained into our economy. Like any other industry, it also means that legislative lag runs deep within the sector. According to the Center of Responsive Politics, Higher Education spent **$82,769,052** in lobbying efforts in 2019. The CollegeBoard, for example, spent nearly $1.5m on lobbying efforts alone in one year, according to the CollegeBoard's 990's Tax Form in 2017.

These lobbying efforts influence the system to greater heights, an example being state-based accountability (SBA). SBA measures school success based on student scores starting with NCLB creation and eventually "Race to The Top", both of which were policy parameters created with the specifications of testing and grades as a significant component. Those tests remained sedentary in a rapidly changing economy and were still bought fast. The SAT or ACT would eventually be a required junior-year test in 23 states across the country.

In an industry where scores meant so much, it also meant that the education system would have to adapt to a higher focus on student grades and scores over loosely experimenting with new ways to record results. The data in education isn't just one in high demand- it's expensive and hard to change.

What this reflects, in greater breadth, is how dependent the higher education industry has become on the system. That system is explicitly rooted in the groundwork of college applications. The critical aspect to note about colleges' applications is that they were designed to reflect data for better quality degrees- better quality is what they had been initially designed for. As a result, what's formed is an industry dependent on data for an economy of years past. This, in turn, becomes the root of lag- from deciding what students learn, how they know it, and how that's reflected.

Vast reform and proposals wouldn't just uproot education- they'd have to end up uprooting how it gets funded, how cities get demand, and what data that depends on. That is not a feat that can be performed by sweeping legislation to solve a problem- but a feat that requires specific, small steps that can adjust different policies accordingly at a given point in time.

This is where startups and lean thinking come into play. While sweeping legislation and the public sector can't fix demand, that doesn't mean that solutions and adaptations can't be found. Those changes are done with fewer targeted problems, with targeted solutions, with data to show and interpret, as we will be exploring in the coming chapters.

In Summary:

- Education isn't simply a public system; it's a gigantic- 1.3 Trillion-dollar industry on its own; it's the business of trading knowledge, from how it's given, to how it's taken, to where, and to why.

- Its fundamental root lies in the college admissions system, which is the primary customer of all the data that public education reflects. As a result, it's also what controls what information is prioritized, appreciated, and highlighted within schools. This, in turn, pushes schools to make ends meet by trying to optimize that data to be as favorable as possible, forming and re-enforcing the way students learn.

- The primary function of the college application is to provide data to colleges: GPA data, testing scores data, student demographic data, student background data, recommendation letters, etc. That data finds its function in helping admission offers predict the students who will likely be the best and profitable fit for the university.

- Students themselves may vary by skills or trade. Still, the result of optimizing the admissions system is both the control the colleges have over what students enter and the ability to discern the best possible student body for them in that year- even before they begin teaching. This puts whatever work they may need to do to grow and raise those students better in their favor.

- A significant aspect of this data comes from testing, which is a massive industry on its own and the materials and relative industries depending on it. This, in turn, means schools that have the best test scores can highlight where students go. Since their funding lies heavily on property taxes, as they can build more significant demand for families through those scores, they can get better funding and improve their infrastructure in a loop.

- That dependency on testing creates a need for high-profile lobbying, where testing companies have been able to put an extensive amount of money into it. They then can push the policies of getting schools to depend more on testing, making them an influential part of school rankings, and even getting them required to be taken in 12 different states. This means that, when needed changes don't serve the interest of companies that hold lobbying power today, the legislation will be hitting multiple lags down the road as corporations get tangled in the fight.

- The lag on its own isn't the problem. But that mismatch in what employers are looking for and what students have comes from not making changes.

- Vast reform and proposals would uproot more than just how students learn. However, small changes being made outside of the public sector indicate an excellent example of how reform can still be effective when done with lean thinking in mind.

Pay me money.

"We need to replace the current model of education with something that doesn't leave people broke for the rest of their lives if it doesn't work out."

How can education clarify its role in the workforce?

"Lambda School doesn't just train people; Lambda School bets on them."

When asked how Lambda School de-risks the pursuit of education for its students, that's the answer that

Austen Allred gives. Allread is the founder of Lambda School, a coding-education platform that teaches data science and full-stack web development. Its teachers consist of engineers from Google, NASA, and MIT. Its students have gone on to get jobs at companies like Apple, Microsoft, Google. The school has also stated that its median graduate salary starts at $70,000, with a placement rate of 79%. It's backed by the likes of VC companies Tandem and Y Combinator. (Lunden 2020), ("Lambda School's 2019 Outcomes Report" 2019)

Lambda students also don't pay any tuition. The deal is simple—and Income Shared Agreement (ISA's) covers tuition unless the student makes $50,000 or more once they get a job. Then, they give a share of their income adjusted for their salary until they meet a $30,000 price cap or until their payment schedule ends.

At any time if the wage dips lower than $50,000, all payments are halted. (Gellman 2018)

Already found the problem within higher education had a lot to do with risk--students would be taking massive amounts of debt, not knowing for sure whether they will be able to manage that debt once they graduate. Sometimes, they don't know whether they'll even be likely to get a job or even how.

I thoroughly believe that the only way the country will be able to move forward and train this and future generations is by not only reducing the cost of higher education but by eliminating the risk of higher education. ***We need to replace the current model of education with something that doesn't leave people broke for the rest of their lives if it doesn't work out. (Allred 2017)***

That risk doesn't stem from the *cost* of higher education; it comes from the crisis of definition that makes it harder to clarify what one really gets when he or she graduates college. What was once an institution designed to give access to exclusive knowledge and train people to be the best in their fields--a compliment to a resume—is now a pathway popularized in chunks by the working class as the route towards general employment. Yet, at the same time, the broad array of selectivity, initial expenditure, and abstract nature of graduation requirements that focus on "well-rounded" students bodes a genuine wonder about what higher education's primary focus is on--institutionalizing the fluid nature of learning or guaranteeing jobs.

That confusion creates a problem, specifically for people who can't afford to take expensive bets on their

career. In his piece, "Why we started Lambda School,"
Allread writes, "...for many people $10,000 is an
unimaginably large amount of money. Not only
because you're not making much, but because close to
every penny of what you *are* making is going into *just
staying alive*." (Allred 2017)

When that confusion isn't there—when someone is
being told *exactly* what they will be learning and *where*
that is designed to take them—there is clarity. All bets
are off. Someone who's pinching pennies can learn how
to build websites spanning the screens of laptops
around the world and get a job out of it, knowing very
well that, if for some reason, they can't pull it off, they
don't have to pay the price for wanting to believe in
themselves. Confidence isn't a treasure box that can be
reached into and transformed magically into a reality.
It's a toddler learning to walk, and sometimes it's going

to need a push to get someone to take the next step. For many students, being confident that they will 'figure it out "once they are out of school doesn't exist securely within them. For many students, knowing where they should expect to end up and what's needed to get there is a core component in building the confidence needed to affirm what they are paying is justified. Because they know where it's going.

Lambda School also doesn't teach like an ordinary school; students repeat units as many times as needed and work in in-house apprenticeships. The school even allows students to become team leaders and learn more about the instructional aspect of building new web applications.

Lambda is not the only school that uses a shared income model. In fact, shared income models are

themselves not a new concept created. In fact, Milton
Friedman proposed this technique of repayment in the
1960s. (Reini 2019)

Praxis, as mentioned before, is another excellent
example of prep school operating under an ISA. Praxis
is a vast education program that sends its students to
apprenticeships, teaches them *how* to learn (not *what* to
learn), and boasts excellent placement rates of its own.

Praxis doesn't specialize in students; instead, *students
specialize themselves.* Once admitted into the program,
students begin to find out what they want to learn--and
spend the first six months building new projects and
expanding their skills. Then they obtain an
apprenticeship with a place of employment where they
can learn under experts, build their resume, and,
eventually, land a job. The students teach themselves,

while Praxis provides a funnel of support for students to drive through- from internships, providing resources, frameworks to learn from, and instructional work designed to help students learn how to learn.

The way students pay their dues to Praxis is also different from that of Lambda. Students pay $2,500 to attend but get delivered back during their internship, where the beginning of an ISA begins once they find work. As they make money by advancing past an apprenticeship, a small share goes to Praxis until the program's cost is fully paid off. ("Praxis | A College Alternative That Leads To A Full-Time Job" n.d.) While not as risk averse as Lambda, the point of Praxis allows people who are either able or more willing to pay to explore more significant paths of passion, a spot to be kick-started through with minimal risk. Isaac

Morehouse, the founder, has a specific idea of what that direction would look like:

"Let's start blogging every day, and let's see if you can get some traffic on some articles and learn what appeals to people, you know, and we're asking them to kind of pick the challenges they want to put in front of themselves, and then we're keeping them accountable to stay on those challenges as they build up a portfolio of projects. Then when it comes time to place them in companies. Now we've got all this stuff to work with. Okay, now you want to pitch this company on hiring you in an entry-level marketing rule, you can share the 30-day blog challenge with them, and you can share with them that you created a landing page. You spent $5 targeting people with a Facebook ad to drive conversions to it, and you fed them a three-email drip sequence. Here you go, here's this thing. I mean, I would love to come work for you; you can showcase."

It's crucial to notice that these platforms don't simply boost everyone up the same way. These institutions were not made to merely enrich minds with the plausibility and pleasure of learning. No, these platforms were made for businesses. They were made to find a way to learn something and use that specific lesson as an asset towards getting a job. It wasn't designed to cater to an elite set of people. These platforms boost the people that want to bet their time and energy towards finding a better career in their lives but aren't attracted to the possibility of putting their entire livelihood onto the line. They want something direct out of what they are doing and take as little risk as needed. They have something set in mind to lift themselves up and to mobilize. For them, a problem in definition can be an end-all or be-all, detracting them from the virtues touted by higher education. The solution is the first step towards education: a clear purpose more affordable than mere curiosity.

That's not to say curiosity is a bad thing; it's certainly not. But doing something for curiosity is a luxury for some. Families need to be fed, pennies are being pinched, and before anything else, a foot that can get someone to the next step of stairs is all that's wanted. They need a chance to start anew, which comes when institutions bet on them the same way they bet on an institution.

In Summary:

- The pursuit of higher education has become a riskier gamble for students. As debt increases and degree placement becomes more and more varied, students get less and less of an idea of where their money is specifically headed when they take on the debt to pursue a degree.

- This issue prompted Lambda founder Austen Allread to create a school that would de-risk the pursuit of education. When it comes to pursuing higher education, Allread states, "*We need to replace the current model of education with something that doesn't leave people broke for the rest of their lives if it doesn't work out.*"

- The problem with the current tuition model doesn't start with *cost*. It begins with a definition. There's no clarification about whether higher education is prioritized for students to get jobs or hone curiosity. From the selection of majors to the way universities market themselves, they've created a massive grey area. This grey area prevents the conversation of how students should pay from appropriately coming into the discussion in the first place.

- Lambda School solved this problem by being specific- telling students what they are learning and for what. As a result, they can put their own skin into the game of student success by utilizing income-shared agreements. It's a coding-education platform that teaches data science and full-stack web development and routes students towards computer-science-specific jobs. Instead of paying tuition, they give a portion of their income to Lambda, which now serves to get students the best possible paying job out of their program. Its median salary and placement rate affirm that success.

- By utilizing ISA's and clarifying their role, students know what they are getting themselves into and use it for a direct expectation, thus de-risking their pursuit of higher education.

- ISAs aren't a new concept- and another example of them being use is Praxis, where students pay $2,500 to attend but get that delivered back during their internship, where a negotiable share of their income goes towards Praxis until paid off. Praxis follows Lambda's model in clarification- directly made for career preparation by helping students teach themselves through apprentices and support programs.

- The primary goal of these institutions isn't to enrich minds- it's to train students for jobs, which is how starting with a problem as small as clarification has led to their success.

Part 2: Stories

Curious Bob.

"I memorized speeches from Mario Cuomo's DNC speech to Braveheart to Jesse Jackson's presidential campaign speeches and recited them over and over again in front of my mirror."

How does education's focus on mastery hinder students from mastering a subject?

Lights. Camera. Action.

"You want me to talk about when I come home at night and my sons ask me what I did today?"

Those are the words spoken by the famed Robert Iger in a trailer he's filming, the CEO of Disney Studios from 2005-2020. He's the man responsible for the acquisitions of Pixar and Marvel, and 21st Century Fox. Under his leadership, Disney made hit movies such as "Frozen," doubled year-on-year revenue and would increase the share price by $100 per share during his tenure. He's the author of the book "Ride of a Lifetime," which documents his life at Disney. (James 2020)

But this isn't a biography about Robert Iger, who also teaches Business Strategy and Leadership on a platform called MasterClass. It's part of his class. That's why he's filming this trailer.

Bob Iger is also not the only notable figure teaching on MasterClass. The platform features some of the world's best-known fields ranging from screenwriting to astrology, including Malcolm Gladwell, Aaron Sorkin, Thomas Keller, Howard Schultz, Gordon Ramsey, and Neil Degrasse Tyson, to name a few.

As you might infer, MasterClass is an online learning platform where you can learn from nationally known experts within a variety of fields, and you'd be mostly correct. While students don't get certificates for their participation in these courses, they still learn the trade tricks to understand their own daily lives.

Learning from the best materials doesn't need to be accredited to be helpful, and that's one of the fundamental roots of founder David Rogier's own existence, who learned to combat stuttering by making great speeches a part of his way to overcome it.

"As a stutterer, one of the most frustrating things is not being able to express myself. When you stutter as you say something, people focus on the stutter, not on the idea you're trying to express. I saw the way people reacted to my stutter. I got a speech therapist and began seriously working on my stuttering. I memorized speeches from Mario Cuomo's DNC speech to Braveheart to Jesse Jackson's presidential campaign speeches and recited them over and over again in front of my mirror."

Rogier- *The Startup*, 2020. (Newnham 2020)

The thing to note here is that, while companies like Praxis and Lambda School have been focusing on the components of finding clarity and purpose in career-training education, MasterClass focuses on the curiosity end and on the abstract. People don't sign up for Masterclass to impress employers; they sign up because they want to listen to how their screenwriter creates a walk-and-talk scene. They sign up for one reason and one reason only--they're curious. As that curiosity breeds, students can begin to venture on their own towards the world of mastery.

The nature of education lies in the wonders that stem from curiosity. Without it, nobody can learn anything because curiosity breeds curiosity. Education is quintessential to bring value to an economic world, but it's also quintessential in acquiring wisdom. How parents guide their children. What it takes to build a better quality of life. Curiosity is the foundation of a child's play. Education, even when it's not taken seriously, is education.

MasterClass solves a more strained gap within formal and informal education, a gap in access to mastery. The schools that can afford experts in their trade can offer more depth for students to quell their curiosities. There's more abstract knowledge to play around with, and students get a much closer pipeline towards the gift of mastery as a result. It's also a story of advantage from youth, and while curiosity will always breed more curiosity, wealth will always generate more wealth. As stated by Yale Law Professor Daniel Markowitz in his article, "American Universities Must Choose: Do They Want to Be Equal or Elite?"

"The elite...send their children to schools that spend many times more on educating their students than middle-class schools: as much as $30,000 per pupil per year for public schools in rich districts and $75,000 per pupil per year at

top private schools, compared to a national public-school median of perhaps $15,000 per year. College and professional school, being dominated by rich children, of course, themselves extend and increase the training gap between the rich and the rest." (Markovits 2019)

Don't be confused. This isn't dissenting commentary on elitism within the US; it's simply a statement that, when there's wealth, more of it can be invested into the next generation, and when it is, some institutions are going to get more resources than others.

Every student can't go to Harvard. But that doesn't necessarily bode mastery exclusivity. In fact, MasterClass isn't a first; books and content creators have existed well before its inception, and the purpose behind Rogier's idea came from something he had learned from his grandmother. "She taught me many things, but one I'll never forget: 'Education is the only thing someone can't take from you.,'" It's what propelled me to create MasterClass and to try to democratize mastery. "

MasterClass isn't a competition to the Ivy League. Any student or person who wants to learn there can. The point is that the barrier to entry is $180, in contrast to the draw of admissions. Students who go to a community college can get one step closer to crafting something special for themselves or getting the opportunity to learn something from the best, simply to pass the time or quell curiosity. The courses aren't the same as what you might find in a university classroom either; the teachers make videos, include supplementary materials for students who are more intrigued, and a discussion board to ask questions and make insights. Simply going to MasterClass won't make someone a master of the greats. Nobody is interacting deeply with the professor, making ally ships, attending guest lectures, or practicing, hands-on, under supervision. But it's the first step. A step that isn't intimidating and one anyone can access, and a step that, done right, can inspire students to take the next ones to lead them to the same paths. It dances with the most active part of learning-the initial curiosity- a spark that otherwise will often be reserved for the places that can afford it the most.

In Summary:

- Mastery is staggered in higher education, with the best institutions that can best offer abstract information and resources that can better lead to developing knowledge of skill towards different students.

- Curiosity plays a foundational role in obtaining mastery- with interest, students can guide themselves toward exploring deeply into topics they desire. But, when access to knowledge is staggered, curiosity's role in education gets displaced from its usual role. As a result, interest becomes harder to hone when students can't have the resources to tap into it.

- Masterclass solves this problem by removing a weighted barrier to entry to access roaringly successful people instructing virtual classes on their given subject.

- People don't sign up to MasterClass because there's a credential to obtain; they sign up because the people they look up to are teaching something they've wanted to learn. In contrast to books, there's also the ability to dive deeper into their work through extra materials and discussions within an organized structure, making MasterClass a pipeline to engage students for the simple purpose of curiosity.

- Going through MasterClass doesn't make a student a master of anything- but the problem being solved isn't a lack of access to mastery. It's making it easier to engage a students' curiosity. It doesn't compete against the Ivy League or Big Ten, or any other large school. Anyone can enter to develop their curiosity and overcome the first hurdle to achieving mastery.

Nano Steps.

"He found that the top-scorers in his class didn't come

from Stanford, but the beaming binary numbers

forming the virtual name of a student learning online."

How can credentials better represent someone's

breadth of knowledge?

Progress is an exciting thing. It's a separate concept

from success entirely, yet it's very often tied into

success. It's not a bridge, but the foundational idea that

the person walking across it is further down than they

were from their previous step. Growing up, progress

was celebrated as its own form of success. Getting a math problem right constituted a high-five, and the faster progress could be made, the more hope would reside in the hearts of both the students and the people seeing them grow.

However, when it came to the world of higher education, progress on its own wasn't a substantial measure in the portrayal of a student's merit. Where they came from to where they were is a story kept to themselves- the distinction of being a fast or strong learner isn't something a transcript or resume can easily portray when the result is what's only being shown. That simplicity has an outstanding level of utility- people get to know what they need to and make quicker decisions in a fast-paced world. At the same time, the pace isn't only dictated by the world. When innovation and imagination are center-stage in the survival of an organization, the ability to learn, adapt, and collect new skills are just- if not more important, than what's already known, simply because the whole point is venturing into the unknown.

Enter Udacity, a tech-teaching platform teaching over 1.6 million students online, partially in through the concept of a "Nanodegree." This is a credential backed and built by industry leaders- donned by more specific skills that, in traditional degree programs, would be part of a more enormous curriculum set, with occasional specialties (such as concentrations), indicated further knowledge. It's gone on to produce a secondary program- the Nanodegree Plus, which guarantees a job within 6 months- or tuition is paid back. In the case of a Nanodegree, that concentration- is-the primary focus. Students can choose to pursue Data Science, AI, Programming, Autonomous Systems,

Cloud Computing, and Business. Rather than indicating a major wrap of knowledge, the Nanodegree shows progress, like how it will demonstrate its "tech stack" (the different systems the program runs on). They take anywhere from 6-12 months, designed to be stepping stones, taking breeding an alternative to the rather abysmal online graduation rates close to 7%- that would exist before its conception.

Udacity isn't led by anyone ordinary, however. Its founder is Sebastian Thurn, a former Stanford Professor (as well as the Founder of Google X, to name two of his accomplishments) who would once teach 200 students to a class. Armed with what was seemingly a dimly competitive epiphany after seeing Sal Khan speak at a TED event he was speaking at; Professor Thun manned the experiment of putting his lectures online. He found that the top-scorers in his class didn't come from Stanford, but the beaming binary numbers forming the virtual name of a student learning online. At that point, the experiment of putting elite-pointed classes online for less money and less time would begin developing. It was an ambitious project, initially designed to be a vast displacement of education, screaming "Reform!" under the mission of putting an Ivy-League tier education on the laptops of the disadvantaged en-masse.

That same experiment's composition- of elite instruction, high accessibility, and quick run forms a rather devastating cocktail, taking the cheers of those combating disadvantage and looking for a fast road to acquire and accredit their skills to work under the vast giant of Big Tech. But it was still missing something. Something didn't taste right.

""I was educating more AI students than there were AI students in all the rest of the world combined." By the end of the semester, he'd raised another $5 million and was standing in front of the Digital Life Design conference in Munich, promising a world in which education was nearly free, available to poor people in the developing world, and better than anything that had come before it. "

It's an opportunity not simply shared by students but the aspect of teaching as well. The high accessibility and progress-oriented utility of Nanodegrees mean that teachers get to play their impact on more students than what they could have once imagined themselves doing.

"I can't teach at Stanford again," he said definitively. "I feel like there's a red pill and a blue pill. And you can take the blue pill and go back to your classroom and lecture your students. But I've taken the red pill. I've seen Wonderland."

Inspiration is potent when in pursuit of progress. The irony, however, is that Udacity failed several times in the quest of finding the correct answer.

It would first find that only 10% of its students would complete its programs, even if the founder himself was teaching the class. Then came the startup's pis-aller: a pivot, leaning onto the grasps of public education to keep itself afloat, allowing its levels to be converted into credits towards state universities in California. There, only 25% of students would pass. Not only was this a class designed by a tenured professor from one of the most competitive universities in the world, but online (where, as mentioned previously, posed a structure that could only boast a 7% success rate). The odds weren't in their favor from the start. It wasn't until the company would court Google to help develop class formation where the company could find its footing. If elite instruction, high accessibility, and quick run time is the perfect mocktail of education credentials, high-industry input was the charismatic barista- selling them on a silver platter.

Trying to take on the Ivy League wasn't the elixir Udacity initially thought it was. Instead, it was able to indicate quick, high-quality, focused progress and skill development. It doesn't compete against the Ivy League anymore. It sidesteps higher education altogether.

Entertain, signal, and give importance to the virtue of progress. Transcripts and degrees are designed for larger bodies of work. Still, when it comes to gigs, progress-oriented work, college-aged students trying to better portray their expertise, and quick launches towards intense software work, the efficiency of a Nanodegree can pose a supplemental solid solution. As reported by Jordan Friedman's article, "What Employers Think of Badges, Nanodegrees from Online Programs,":

"in one recent survey of 114 human resources managers across various industries, only 5 percent said they weren't interested in digital badges at all, though this didn't include badges exclusively from online programs. Sixty-two percent of the respondents said they were interested in badges..." (Friedman, 2016)

The regal elegance of extracting the power of progress to show what one's capable of comes from its effectiveness. If there is any case study that can verify that full circle, it's Udacity.

In Summary:

- The focus on education credentials is on what's being known- but without acknowledging progress and indicating a candidate's ability to improve and learn skills.

- Udemy solved this by making a credential designed to funnel students and be an indicator of student improvement and knowledge.

- When it came to the world of higher education, progress on its own wasn't a substantial measure in the portrayal of a student's merit. Where they came from to where they were is a story kept to themselves- the distinction of being a fast or strong learner isn't something a transcript or resume can easily portray when the result is what's only being shown. That simplicity has an outstanding level of utility- people get to know what they need to and make quicker decisions in a fast-paced world.

- Enter Udacity, a tech-teaching platform teaching over 1.6 million students online, partially in through the concept of a "Nanodegree," or a credential backed and built by industry leaders.

- It would first find that only 10% of its students would complete its programs, even if the founder himself was teaching the class. It wasn't until the company would court Google to help develop class formation where the company could find its footing.

- Nanodegrees have posed a strong interest in recruitment. Udacity, in that regard, found it's an experiment to be a substantial success.

When Computers

Exist.

"With modern day computing, the computational limit

that humans initially had, no longer exists."

What is modern-day math education missing?

"Our mission is to reconceptualize the mainstream

mathematics curriculum by assuming computers exist."

It's a line with an appealingly cynical wit, proposing

the jaw-dropping revelation of acknowledging the

obvious. It's also the front-page quote of computerbasedmath.org, the domain for "The Maths Fix," a book offering to change the way students practice and teach mathematics. Its author is Conrad Wolfram, a middle-aged British man who's also the co-founder of Wolfram Research and his brother, who formed a mathematical computational engine bearing the name Wolfram-Alpha.

Wolfram Alpha is, in some ways, the quintessential life hack for the modern math student stumped by the math on question #4. As a Google for math equations, a student can type in a math problem- including complex polynomials, derivatives, or quadratic functions, to name a few, get the answer, as well as the step-by-step process to how it's done. It's a tool that has every reason to instill worry as much as rejoice to the hearts of teachers around- while it's great that there's an engine that can help students when they're stuck, it also allows the students who haven't computed anything yet to—well—compute.

Strangely, that's Wolfram's whole point. "Calculating is the machinery of math - a means to an end," said Wolfram, in his TedX speech, "Teaching kids real math with computers. The talk centers around a simple concept regarding math education - that the teaching of math shouldn't be centered around computational ability, but computational thinking. The argument does that mathematics had one human limit to how far it's exploration could be driven, which was calculating. It's not typical to see a mind that can solve abstract polynomial equations in the blink of an eye, but with modern day computing, the computational limit that humans initially had, no longer exists." (TED 2010)

As a result, the exploration around finding numerical representation in an abstract world is an outstanding opportunity from a teaching context. This is a world where scientists, engineers, physicists, and worlds alike have a greater focus on asking the right questions that make up the correct answer, in contrast to finding the right solution.

"You don't necessarily need to learn every step needed to solve a quadratic equation. You probably need to know what a quadratic equation is. You need to know how to set up the equation...but most crucially, you need to know when you're going to set up an equation, and why—which very few people coming out of school actually know." (TED 2010)

Wolfram's problem is that, when it comes to how math is being taught right now, implementation and conceptualization in a world where high-powered computing is the standard-bearer of mathematical solutions across industries are limited in instruction. Calculus, for example, which begins with the concept of limits towards 0, is taught primarily in higher-level education, mainly in part to the more complex computational demand it encounters. But, if the computational market was more stripped down-if the computation could be automated, the concepts could be explored earlier. Learning the foundational concepts and real-world applications of, say, finding the area underneath a curve. Rather than focusing on solving the problem, students would focus on asking the right questions, leading to the correct equation, getting the answer, then discussing and experimenting with its implications.

More simply put, math education is facing the focus on computing the correct answer when computation is easily accessible by most, making the direction bear far less use than what it once had. By lifting away from that focus and more towards how the problem is solved (from asking the right question to making the proper interpretations), Wolfram adapts the power of mathematics to an era where computing is vastly more automated.

It's a small solution, but it dives right into the main problem in math education- not that it's ineffective, but that the focus is aimed at a skill that doesn't deliver the return it once did when computation had to be done by hand. It's not all-expansive.

Wolfram changes this by focusing on the expansive. The right questions, thinking, and interpretation. A small change- a mind-shift- that can take that problem away.

Vast computation gives access to a world of tactile experimentation, a strong point of relevant engagement for students to learn more thoroughly off-of. The nature of tactile implementation is also what led to Wolfram's love for mathematics in the first place. He says, "I wasn't interested in the actual structure of it and how it worked. What really interested me was applying it in physics or in other areas." (Wan 2018)

The misconception that's coming out of schools is that when students learn algebra, they take it with them until the final and then forget all about it, but it doesn't necessarily need to be the case. When the focus runs on concepts, the applications of mathematics indeed can be pulled to the extent of one's imagination. For example, when building a contraption for a marble race, students can get the incline they desire by finding the slope to give them its desired speed and apply trigonometric ratios to complete the job.

However, when the system rears its head through computation as the primary focus, implementing mathematics into the abstract worlds of imagination isn't as clearly implemented. As stated by Professor James Stigler in Stuart Wolpert's paper, "Why so many U.S. students aren't learning math," Wolpert says "We teach math as disconnected facts and as a series of steps or procedures — do this, and this and this — without connecting procedures with concepts, and without thinking or problem-solving. "Don't just memorize it and spit it back on the test." (Wolpert, 2018.)

Is this to say the curriculum does away with computational thinking altogether? No. Estimates are done off the top of one's head; arithmetic and calculating prowess aren't foreign to the human mind. They're natural, and they're innate. But they have a new place in life now, as a foundational part of instinct, thinking on one's feet and putting the numbers of the world in front of their own eyes. However, its consequential limits can be set aside while still carrying the benefit of summing things up in a moment's notice.

It's that simplicity that Wolfram Alpha drives itself on—the fact that these answers are readily available. It's not a school, a training program, or a math learning course. It's a simple way to ask mathematical questions. But some of education's most important tools haven't come from an institution—they come from places where the right questions can get the correct answers, like Google.

Google made it so that the limits that come from a human's capacity to memorize facts no longer existed, and so forth came a wave of being able to learn, adapt, and fit different concepts together to build an ecosystem the world can no longer live without. In essence, Wolfram Alpha is an outlet towards that freedom while also allowing the potential for far more advanced problems with the right concepts to flourish in a new, more powerful way, like a central puzzle piece perfectly made to fit.

Reforming math isn't about making profound, creative changes to a system imprinted onto this world before the conception of 0. It's about knowing what tools exist and using them to solve problems, the way math should do in the first place.

In Summary:

- The problem with math education comes from the fact that it doesn't acknowledge how computers have changed how we can explore the world of mathematics, meaning students don't get to explore the more significant opportunities that come from automated computation. While there's a place for computational thinking, it's lying more in instinct and quick-thinking work than robust application.

- Computation in mathematics is a fundamental process in finding the correct answer, but that doesn't mean it needs to be done all through the head. There isn't a rule in the workforce prohibiting mathematicians from using computers- and as such, they are. Wolfram-

Alpha solves this by acknowledging that change in education, which in turn, shifts students away from trying to memorize formulas to the other parts of finding the answer- like asking the right questions, using the correct thinking process, and being able to interpret the results.

- Wolfram-Alpha, however, straightforwardly does this- it's an engine that does heavy computation with the ease of just plugging in the problem.

- Some of education's most important tools haven't come from an institution—they come from places where the right questions can get the correct answers, like Google.

- Wolfram-Alpha's solution is a simple one, but it's a great demonstrator of lean thinking and getting down to finding the right problem to solve.

The Point Of

Growth

"In wealthier districts, including those in the northern suburbs, teachers received much more training and support."

How can education form better goals?

The goalposts of education seem simple enough. It's accumulating knowledge and being able to find a way to apply it in one's life. The primary goals for assessing results are to reflect how well one has shown their ability to absorb said knowledge on a quiz, essay, or school project- it's what student rankings, scores, and course levels all, in some part indicate. Taking an honors course means that there's more depth to school material. A 4.0 suggests that students have remembered a vast amount of knowledge according to their courses. At a larger scale, class rankings indicate how those scores compare and which students know more.

It's hard to deny a core truth about knowledge and education--the mark of successful teaching finds much of its bearing on how well the student can reflect on their instruction. However, the goalposts in which that's done, specifically in K-12 education, aren't necessarily the only goalposts needed to make the game successful. An example of this comes from The Common Core's College and Career Readiness Anchor

Standards for Reading for K-5 education, in which the key objectives include:

- *1. Read closely to determine what the text says explicitly and make logical inferences from it; cite specific textual evidence when writing or speaking to support conclusions drawn from the text.*
- *2. Determine central ideas or themes of a text, analyze their development, summarize the key supporting details and pictures.*
- *3. Analyze how and why individuals, events, and ideas develop and interact throughout a text.*

What you'll notice about these standards is that they are action and result based. The students are expected to make logical inferences, cite evidence, find central ideas, track development, and understand the more intricate intents behind a text. The expectation is to make a good argument.

Simply put, the goal's frame around the students can find and make a case for interpretations in their reading. Those goals, however, lack the fundamental point of growth. Notice that these goals aren't about improvement. The focus isn't being increasingly less reliant on instructor assistance while interpreting and arguing with text. While these standards are progressive- in the sense that they build up year after year, the specific coursework in a class consists of learning goals that don't focus on improvement.

The indicator comes with the end goal: that the students can learn further on their own and are better off than where they were before under that core frame of making the excellent argument mentioned above.

Rather than focusing on whether the view is good, the focus is on whether or not it has gotten better since the first time. It's important to remember that students start at different places, meaning they are more likely than not to end up in other destinations.

In contrast to this, the learning goals behind Common Core, by focusing on results, don't allow flexibility of circumstances to be a feasible part of measuring student success. Students come from different homes with different skills and different resources to work around. The factors student scores depend on far more than how well a teacher can teach- and when the goalposts for measuring student and school success depend on static scores, student achievement falls flat.

Susie Ans' and Arriana Cardona-Maguigad's piece,
"Common Core: Higher Expectations, Flat Results,"
explores the problems from the start- such as the
inadequacy in training support. As stated in their
interview with Tom Loveless, a former fellow at The
Brooking Institute,

"...the police didn't take into account socioeconomic
differences. Some schools in Illinois are clear examples
of that. Like Chicago Public Schools, teachers say they
had a hard time transitioning in less-resourced districts
because of a lack of coordination. In wealthier districts,
including those in the northern suburbs, teachers
received much more training and support."

The tests the curriculum works with in the first place
have shown lackluster improvement. An example of
this comes from the IAR (Illinois Assessment of

Readiness), which, in 2019, showed that only 38% of the kids passed the English exam, and just 32% met expectations in math.

That's an average rate of just 35%- a little over 1/3. In Illinois, even after adopting Common Core- only 1/3 of students hit those expectations. Generally, the argument is that the Common Core is simply ineffective. But what if, instead, it's merely focusing on the wrong things?

You'll notice a central commonality in programs like Praxis, Lambda, Khan Academy, and Masterclass between all the programs and solutions. The students have a significant role in how they are taught, with a substantial component of these projects being that students focus heavily on learning *how* to learn, not simply *what* to learn. The focus is on progress, in contrast to static results.

It's also the central theme of Matt Bordeau's micro-school (one-room schoolhouse) K-12 program, Acton Academy Placer. "Very early on our five-year-old are setting their own personal goals right; they set daily goals and proprietary software they're learning to keep track of their goals and get better than they were yesterday." As simple as it might be, that theme of setting goals early on can go a long way, and they get reflected right in the school itself.

"Everybody has real jobs. They have real work that they have to do, and they're really accountable to other people on them, picking their jobs, designing their jobs, everything from the bathrooms getting cleaned to the quality of the food that gets cooked for lunches for everybody it's done by students. "

The foundation of their curriculum comes from separating the individual from the collective, where students get input in their learning plans and take personal ownership towards getting there and have behavioral contracts that they need to uphold. Those foundations mean that to keep succeeding at a school like Acton Placer, students need to holistically evaluate themselves as much as possible to achieve as others consider them and find the spots, they need to achieve growth.

At the point where self-awareness becomes the principal, the bar for learning changes. The focus is no longer on simply where a student is, but how they got there and whether they are at a point where they can get to more places without the help of an adult. Those kids get the advantage of adapting, disarm, and using failure as a steppingstone towards a more remarkable victory. It's the formation of motivation arising from the confidence that they can do it, at some point and in some way.

Matt is also not the only person who runs an Acton Academy. Acton is a micro-school network. Parents and teachers get the supplies needed to help run a one-room school, with the teaching style centered around student accountability.

Students have so much control over their learning that they can even choose the types of technology tools they use and can propose new tools when they find them. Central to the entire process of picking and choosing technology is the idea that students are the ones who know their learning best, and therefore, should be the ones calling the shots on purchasing decisions. - EdSurge, 2015.

The overarching theme of Acton Academy is quite ambitious. It's the center stage of what more foundational changes in education (specifically, curriculums) are. Students find higher callings, take apprenticeships, follow role models, follow primarily through "quests"- or long-term projects. They take on formal, open-ended discussions every day and work on skills based on the time they set for themselves. It's accountability and the application of it on steroids.

The truth is it might be overly ambitious. The level of changes that Acton Academy places onto its teaching style is immense, and it's not something that easily fits into the sector of public education. It would require a rather drastic upheaval in the pipeline for jobs, change the way schools expect to run, and fundamentally uproot the interaction and requirements. Sacrifices teachers would have to make to emulate such a concept. But by shifting the goalposts of their educational goals, Acton Academy can create a system that can begin to assess skills that can't as easily be measured in Academia but can matter heavily to how a child will interact with the market world as they grow older.

In Tom Foster's Article, Inside the Schools That Want to Create the Next Mark Zuckerberg, Foster speaks to Victor Hwang, the VP of Kauffman Foundation, who outlines the very same problem, stating:

" The U.S. beats itself up and says our math and science scores are testing lower than other countries', and we should focus on that, but it doesn't play to the advantages the U.S. has. Where the U.S. has excelled is in finding answers where there's ambiguity. The challenge is that there are no good established metrics for that. How do you measure creative instinct or entrepreneurship, coming up with a product that nobody else thought was possible? That's what these programs are moving toward addressing. "

Acton Academy hasn't been short on its success' either. The network has around 150 schools spanned across the world, set from Lansing, Michigan, to Guatemala City. Its price to open costs $15,000 and costs 3% of year-on-year revenue after that.

The note that's to be taken heavily from this doesn't come from Acton Academy's ambitious reaches or its radical new system; It's about the first step it took-shifting the goalposts from what's learned to the accomplished. It's through establishing that goal in which these radical experiments could find a home, but this capacity isn't limited to the changes Acton wanted to bring. Acton enabled the possibility of more flexible adaptation by changing the goalposts, and loose adaptation doesn't mean sweeping reform. It means flexible adaptation. It gives the freedom for changes to be explored and keep adapting, just like what it's intended to do with students.

It's a tiny change of the mind, but it yields more extensive results.

In Summary:

- The goalposts in the public education sphere focus on measures of student success that have dependencies outside the classroom.

- Those goalposts create inconsistencies in measuring the effectiveness of the right programs, meaning the straightforward goals education puts heads in a less productive direction. An example of this is The Common Core's College and Career Readiness Anchor Standards for Reading for K-5 education. The key objectives aim for how well a student can argue and interpret a text in the end, without regard for where they begin.

- How well a student can fundamentally score is highly varied and based on many external factors a school cannot easily control, making the process of measuring their quality flawed by prioritizing static results, thus forming flawed interpretations.

- However, this problem's solution is the simple concept of shifting the goalposts- where, instead of focusing on the endpoint of students, there's a focus on where they start and how they improve. The programs mentioned in this book in previous chapters have a common theme to them in which the students play a significant role in teaching themselves.

- Acton Academy puts this concept front-and-center, where students set their own goals every day- and a primary focus stays on improvement. This model has shown some success for Academy, which has around 150 schools spanned worldwide, set from Lansing, Michigan to Guatemala City.

- While Acton Academy on its own has ambitious notes, its crucial starting point is simply solving the problem by changing how it looks at achieving goals.

Children Left

Behind.

"An analyst working within hedge-fund finance would take the bet of living on his savings for nine months."

How does focusing on scores leave students behind?

In some ways, it sounds like a redemptive tale. An Ivy-League hedge fund hotshot takes the risk of educating millions of students online, starting with his family. Fast forward a couple of years, and he's a world-famed teacher, creating lessons that stem from High School Algebra to Art History.

His name is Sal Khan, and he's the founder of the non-profit Khan Academy, an educational experiment test surrounding online-based, no-pressure- failure, educational achievement platform, turned-to startup success story.

There are many levers where one could reimagine education, but the one that we focus most on is on this notion of, in a traditional academic model, kids move ahead at a fixed pace. A teacher will cover a topic for a couple of weeks, and then there'll be an assessment. And on that assessment, one student gets 70 percent, another student gets 80 percent, another student gets 95 percent, and even though the evaluation identified those gaps, the class will then move on to the next concept. Those gaps keep accumulating.

Classes keep moving. There's a regimen- a pace, a pace locked on heels. It doesn't slow down, and it's a pace everyone is expected to come up, and it creates a bigger problem. When students fall behind on a lesson topic, they have to find a way to recover that, or in time, they grow more and more behind, left increasingly confused about the lesson topics that continue. The thing is, students might miss class. Students might not learn effectively in the course. Students might not know at that exact place. The students that can make up for that can move onto the next topic, and for them- the relentless pace works fine. But the relentless pace becomes a disservice to a whole other group of kids.

The kids who get left behind. 70% of community college students are taking remedial math courses. The students who fall asleep in class because they have work until 8 PM after school. The students don't learn from lectures but pictures or tactile methods.

Curriculums move fast, and knowledge accumulates. Pre-tested or not, the end goal has to be to get everyone with a similar purpose of knowing the skills in a set amount of time. In some sense, it's a consequence of the efficiency that testing provides towards students, teachers, and colleges alike. While testing offers a comparative, simple gauged- data point, it also forms the goals of the curriculum, and grading reflects what students know. There isn't an out.

More than 50 percent of students entering two-year colleges and nearly 20 percent of those entering four-year universities are in remedial classes. For community college students, almost 4 in 10 end up not completing those classes themselves. Not only are students retaking courses that they weren't able to grasp in high school, but those courses also often end up not working in the first place.

Courses not working indicates a much more critical takeaway- its better students are thorough with their learning over them trying to leap ahead, only to loop back around.

It also produces the problem that makes all the difference in who can score and who cannot. But what happens when something isn't understood? Teachers are human with limited sets of time to help. Tutors have schedules they need to follow. If something isn't understood, it compounds when students in the class get taught the same thing. Throw learning gaps in, and there isn't a standard procedure for how learning gaps level in the classroom.

Khan Academy, on the other hand, is a program that's been clear-cut. Students start with pre-made lectures on the micro-units of the topic, generally following standard K-12 and AP curriculum procedures. Once those videos finish, students can gauge what they know through practice quizzes where they need to answer three answers in a row to complete the lesson. Emphasize the **practice.**

There are two core benefits to this technique. Students can find the specific topic that is bugging them and progress from there, instead of having to start the unit over from scratch, which gives a standard direction for addressing gaps. The pressure of failure is also heavily lifted because students don't worry about **what** they know. The score is for **knowing** it whenever they do. Suppose a student wants to learn about Finance and Capital markets, but they got stuck on stocks in class. In that case, Khan Academy allows them to catch up by drilling them on the basics of stocks until they've demonstrated they finally understand it. They don't move onto ETF's, Index Funds, or more complex financial lingo until a student can fully understand that a stock is a security representing a specific amount of ownership in a corporation.

The emphasis on this is on the procedure. Khan Academy sets the basis for **how** students will curb knowledge gaps. It doesn't simply let the problem exist, entrusting that part of the job is to find a solution - it provides a method everybody can access, with the sole intent being that the lessons' personalization at the students' pace is the way that gap can shrink. When students go to Khan Academy, they know why, and they know how this works. Khan Academy doesn't pressure students to get to a certain level of knowledge or depend on grades to carry its results forward. It takes itself based on a simple solution- allowing students to curb learning gaps.

The student indicated how much they could learn, at what point, and when. The pressure is off, while the solution doesn't change. It's that mindset shift that becomes the ignition for student growth. As Khan stated in an interview with HBR,

The one meta-level thing is to take agency over your learning. In the traditional academic model, you're passive. You sit in a chair, and the teacher tries to project knowledge at you; some of it sticks, some of it doesn't.

That's not an effective way to learn. Worse, it creates a mindset of "you need to teach me," so when you're on your own, you think, "I can't learn."

The students guide the fixing of their gaps. At the same time, Khan Academy gives them the material to do so and the ability to vary the intuition of confidence that is the core mark of confirmation a student will rely on when asked whether they know something.

The experiment of Khan Academy is a notorious success, backed by philanthropists of caliber, such as Bill Gates or Carlos Slim. It has racked up 100 million users and worked closely with California School districts to utilize their program to uplift 40% of students who couldn't afford SAT tutoring to raise scores high enough to apply to state-level universities. It's a solution whose most basic concept started with tutoring Khan's cousin, Nadia, long-distance through the phone.

The success of that trial triggered a chain reaction. Word would get around. Eventually, Khan would begin posting videos on YouTube- because once he was helping more and more students fix gaps they missed in class. It would become harsher and tougher to schedule classes, especially working full-time as a Hedge Fund analyst.

The classic problem of tutorship was the same problem mentioned earlier in the chapter—those twisted schedules that can stop tutors in their tracks. Khan solved it. But he didn't solve it by trying to find the correct answer- but the right problem, that problem being that kids who get left behind, stay behind. He solved it with a simple solution- focus on them being able to understand what they need to before they move onto the next topic- a focus on the slight problem, starting with a lean solution.

As the presence of his teaching could expand further and further, thanks to the scalability put forward by his work, the crossroads would come - whether he'd have to plunge into some financial risk to do that. At that point, an analyst working within hedge-fund finance would take the bet of living on his savings for nine months. Then, in October of 2010- Khan Academy would find itself forming its first office.

Fast forward a decade, and Sal Khan was dubbed as "The World's Teacher," and is spinning off a second experiment in student reform—Khan Lab School. It's a school focused on Mastery-Based Learning, where students get whatever time they need to complete a course, brimmed with mixed-age cohorts. Once they have shown mastery in that specific course, they can move onto the next one- a domino effect rising a staircase of progression. It emphasizes building social skills and hands its vitality towards project-based learning.

It is said that 65% of children who enter school now will end up working in jobs that don't yet exist. So what does this mean for educational systems? We can no longer teach students the way we have in the past, focusing on the passing of knowledge from the teacher to the student. If we truly want to prepare students to solve the problems of the future, ***then we need to give them real problems to solve***

The test has consisted of 200 students and is rather new, but it's not Khan's first experiment. Like Khan

Academy, the view of thorough progression is the foundation of how Khan Academy found its success. It could very well be a foundation of what takes Khan Lab Schools to whatever next step it sets its eyes on, with the keen optimism of a student that knows that they know what they're doing.

In Summary:

- Strict paces aimed towards specific scores have the capacity to and does- put kids who misunderstood or missed crucial topics crucially left behind for advancement.

- Due to student testing and specific end-measures being the endpoint for many classes, moving at a constant pace for students is integral to the course's success and the school. As much as teachers and tutors will want to make sure their students learn pretty, they don't have all the time and resources to do that atop ordinary teaching day by day. It also produces the problem that makes all the difference in who can score and who cannot.

- Khan Academy solves this by emphasizing micro topic practice- where the student does not move forward within a section unless they have demonstrated that they can adequately understand and comprehend everything within that microscope.

- The emphasis on this is on the procedure. Khan Academy sets the basis for **how** students will curb knowledge gaps. It doesn't simply let the problem exist, entrusting that part of the job is to find a solution- it provides a method everybody can access, with the sole intent being that the personalization of the lessons, at the student's pace, is the way that gap can shrink.

- The students guide the fixing of their gaps. At the same time, Khan Academy gives them the material to do so the intuition of confidence that is the core mark which a student will rely on when asked, whether they know something, allowing students to depend less on teachers and tutors over time.

- The experiment of Khan Academy is a notorious success, backed by philanthropists of caliber, such as Bill Gates or Carlos Slim. It has racked up 100 million users and worked closely with California School districts to utilize their program to uplift 40% of students who couldn't afford SAT tutoring to raise scores high enough to apply to state-level universities.

Part 3: Policy

Better Grades.

"Learning is a process that begins with amateur knowledge and extends itself into matured mastery."

How do policy-based proposals, like standards-based, present themselves to the public?

In Part II, I detailed the trials of secret experiments solving public problems. The success behind those secret experiments was the fact that there's a lot less to push through. For them, changes don't need to appeal to more sets of people than consumers. It's not partisan, and there isn't a long, complex, strike-down process that must consider a massive ring of problems well outside the scope of education, as policies. But when policy does get passed, these decisions can affect the vast or the specific. It has a range private sector don't. The policy has the power to control. It can elevate success quickly, a power that makes the pen mightier than the sword. It afflicts change in ways private sectors can't without the caffeinated force of money shielding it from the woes of failure. The government has money; it's a bully pulpit, and it can push things.

Now, there's the debate as to whether an institution should HAVE that type of power, but it's hard to deny the fact that it does, currently, uphold that level of control. With that power comes the ability to notice new ideas and push them to the public on a larger scale, such as policies that dictate grading for students.

There's something else consistently to be noted about private solutions - the traditional grading system doesn't have much of a home in them. That's not to say that, simply because those successes don't use it, a school system that finds a core part of its dependency and data reflection through the first four letters of the alphabet should quickly abolish it in the name of being all that is moral and good. Education, publicly, is a system. Its normal operations holistically depend on an efficient way of streamlining data and filtering success towards failure. Grades are a part of that.

Despite that, noting what could contribute to successful programs and proposing a solution based on its foundations isn't a rare phenomenon for improvement to accustom. Thus, there exists a proposal that differentiates itself from traditional

Grading- Standards-Based Grading. While grades still have the simplicity of letters for data collection, the Grading goes a different process.

As described by Robert J. Marzano and Tammy Heflebower in their paper, "Grades That Show What Students Know," Marzano and Heflebower represent the overall strategy of standards-based Grading.

The strategy is "A variation on this theme is to keep track of percentage scores across various categories of performance and behavior and then translate the average percentage score into a letter grade or simply report the average percentage score (for example, 62.9 percent)."

The specifics of Standards-Based Grading have a fundamental difference in contrast to ordinary

Grading- the basis is made more heavily towards learning goals. Those goals are more substantive but less in volume, and student progress is more imperative towards Grading. It works similar to a rubric, where students know what they need to achieve their desired grade early on within the lesson. Students have a starting point now- as well as an ending point. Students will usually have initial scores indicating where they start, the scale being 1-4.

Expectedly, one represents novel understanding, while 4 indicated a level of mastery. The student's goal is to raise their scores from where they began, not continuously score high points to demonstrate knowledge. The elements of failure lay the groundwork for progress towards mastery.

A somewhat rigid example of this could be in a hypothetical English class. Students are handed a rubric during the beginning of a lesson, stating the expectation of mastery. The work then centers around one central essay for a more prolonged period as students slowly build their writing. They raise their overall score from a 1 to a 3.5 when the lesson and final paper completes.

In this grading system, students don't worry about the qualms of learning. Learning is a process that begins with amateur knowledge and extends itself into matured mastery. Where one starts isn't where that one ends up staying when the mind becomes enriched. It amplifies the audacity of risk, for asking questions, and for exploring. Grading students through standards over numerical results drive that forward. It gives an incentive for a kid to ask a question, admit they don't know something and work towards righting their wrongs.

The core part of standards-based Grading isn't about the changes in Grading; it's the changes in mindset. It positions itself as marking clear communication with students- expectations, what they did wrong, and what needs to improve. The student response, not by saying "I know that," or by marking a question right on a quiz, it's by correcting their mistakes, eventually to the point of autonomy. How teachers and students work with each other becomes closer to an equal partnership than a test towards how good both parties are. As middle School Administrator Joshua Wolf published his own experiences, Wolf emphasized the communicative shift, stating, "Standards-based Grading allows me to clearly communicate with students and parents where individuals are with their understanding of each concept. No longer are students able to hide behind weighted averages and positive academic behaviors such as attendance."

That part about attendance perks many ears as well. What messages are kids talking about when they don't get penalized for not showing up? More than that- why would the discipline that schools bring in be so relaxed? What happens when kids get taught that they don't always need to try their best the first time around? How do people find time to implement this? Is behavior and how they get their work done as-if not more important than whether they get it done in the first place?

The point is, like any idea, Standards-Based Grading isn't short of its flaws either. Teacher Baptist Devalle, for example, found the consequences of striking damage as students become of age:

Here's how I explain it to my students: If you're asked to meet a deadline in a future job, and you're late or have poor-quality work, you might get fired. If you're in a relationship and don't show up to the dates, you might get dumped. If you cross the road without looking, and a car comes zooming by, you don't get a second chance."

It takes effect into a broader type of discussion- that if kids have the freedom to show up, as long as they get their work don't, is it a problem? When it comes to trying their best- is it about the result, with discretionary effort, or building the habit of hard work from the get-go? If the behavior isn't a significant impact on a student's ability to work, and the method (so long as it's fair) gets the work done, what's the worry? There's the sentiment that students wouldn't be absent of these lessons in the first place with a new perspective on teaching either, that rules about behavior, attendance, and effort don't need to fade away- but rather put themselves strictly into the boxes of conduct.

The conversation about standards-based Grading isn't just about reflecting results; it's reflecting on what education needs to be valuing the most. The data behind pilot programs have built a rally of support, emphasized by the research primer, "What does the research say about standards-based grading?", by Matt Townsley & Tom Buckmiller:

While studying standards-based pilot programs in Kentucky, Guskey, Jung, and Swan (2011) found teachers and families nearly unanimous in their agreement that standards-based reports provided better and clearer information. Thus, the power of SBG lies in the opportunity for a more nuanced and focused conversation between parents and teachers about where students are strong, where they are weak, and how each can help the student (Spencer, 2012).

More locally, in a survey conducted by District 49, 72% of surveyed teachers saw it as a better way to reflect the knowledge,
while 83% of surveyed parents disagreed. The idea of reforming how a kid gets graded isn't one that a parent can be immediately receptive to at the end of the day; it's their child! For some parents, if their child is doing fine in school- what's the problem? For others, it can be the fact that- they don't know what's going into the grades their students are taking. For others, it could be the fact that they didn't grow up with it. It's uncharted territory and having their child be a test subject for a proposal that isn't unanimous is a rather large bet for a

parent. The idea meets with skepticism, as for many, it likely should and would be. After all, these aren't lab rats. They're children of a parent.

So there comes the state of the proposal- a divided work in progress. Teachers yet can't verify its effectiveness, nor can parents boost for change. But it's a solution to a plaguing problem in academics- it exchanges efficiency for depth. It has more data points to uphold, and it shifts the mindset towards consistent advancement. Most of all, it makes things clear for both the parent and the student. Standard-based Grading proposes solving the miscommunication, pressure, and more minimal data points traditional Grading offers as a survey of knowledge is significant.

Why? Because, when its mere existence can spark and maintain its end of the conversation, it, and like a

student mastering a new concept, can be autonomous
incoming towards the solution through its own.

In Summary:

- The state of the proposal of standards-based
  Grading is in a pivotal moment- whether it can
  focus on simply solving the problems it's made
  to solve, or if it extends into bolder tasks and
  policy sweeps that detract its progress.
- The problem Standards-Based-Grading aims to
  solve is the lack of fortified data from the
  current grading system enabled today by
  enabling a new, progress-based grading system
  that captures more points from the beginning to
  the end, centralizing on progress over the
  endpoint.

- Standards-Based Grading, on its own, is a proposal to solve the miscommunication, pressure, and more minimal data points traditional Grading offers as a survey of knowledge- before being a mainstream grading system on its own.

- When policy does get passed- and how it can get passed, its decisions can affect the vast or the specific. It has a range private sectors don't. The policy has the power to control. It can elevate success quickly, a power that makes the pen mightier than the sword. It afflicts change in ways private sectors can't do without the caffeinated force of money shielding it from the woes of failure. The government has money; it's a bully pulpit, and it can push things.

- The score goes from 1, which is novel understanding, while 4 indicates a level of mastery. The student's goal is to raise their scores from where they began, not continuously score high points to demonstrate knowledge. The elements of failure lay the groundwork for progress towards mastery.

The Project.

"They explore the world's facets with the tips of their tongue, the pupils of their eyes, the drums of their ears."

How do large-scale learning projects incorporate mindshifts in the way they carry change?

Project-based learning isn't a proposal that can be defined as a conservative approach in any sense of the term. It fundamentally changes the way students learn. Initially, it seems like a counter-intuitive point to include in a book that's spent the past 12 chapters arguing the case for a more conservative, small step mindset towards complementing new education policies in the US.

But this book wouldn't be making its case if it didn't present an example of the gains and the drawbacks that more sweeping visions of changing education look like. It also wouldn't be making its case if it couldn't find that, even with a reformist method as sweeping as project-based learning, it stems from the Mindshifting approach referred to in this book in the first place.

The scope of project-based learning. It isn't hard to understand. It's a learning methodology that sticks to its name, and its premise is that kids do real-world work.

While its effects are radical, the idea behind it isn't. Kids being hands-on to learn is a natural strategy that's stood with children since they were babies. It's a strategy that's been a part of education since very early on. PBL was established in 1907 through the discovery of an educator by the name of Maria Montessori. She opened a high-quality daycare center for disadvantaged students. She would soon find "The children were unruly at first, but soon she'd great interest in entering with puzzles, learning to prepare meals, and manipulate lemony materials Maria had designed." She observed how the children absorbed knowledge from their surroundings, essentially teaching themselves.

Project-based learning isn't new but any means. Its techniques are standard since babies learn heavily from their environment through sensory and exploration. They explore the world's facets with the tips of their tongue, the pupils of their eyes, the drums of their ears. They explore. They interact. They play.

The effectiveness standard for project-based learning is not bodingly unnatural or unsuccessful. In Peter Glenn's piece, "Why Project Based Learning hasn't gone mainstream," Glen explores the more monumental successes of project-based learning, stating that "Some project based schools report 20% higher standardized test scores than those with conventional classrooms". (Glen, 2019)

The kids do better- even within the core system already constructed. In fact, it sounds like project-based learning could, in fact, have been the standard, with its effectiveness showing a greater capacity for success before the complete advent of the system, with the grassroots of the education industry already being formed in its own space.

In fact, outside of public education, project-based learning is a formidable component of many programs, including Lambda and Praxis. Yet, even though it poses such promise, only 1% of schools actually commit to using project-based learning. 1%. The reason why is because it's positioned itself as a big ask.

For one thing, it takes longer to work with, plain and simple. "In a recent survey teachers using crowd school reported that even after significant training it can initially take 3 times more one to plan and organize projects than teaching with a traditional lecture and test format."

Schools don't just teach students; it sends them away when the parents aren't home. Buses come early so parents can see their kids, and ousting school activities, kids generally come back around the same time as a workday. You'd need to restructure the entire workday to pull in all the gains project-based learning proposes. Or, you could begin working with parents to become comfortable with their children being home when they might not be (or vice versa).

That's not to mention that teachers make about $60K a year on average, and the ask is to pull 3 times the time investment to make the changes happen, forcing schools to further have to negotiate funding conversations. Or, the focus initially starts with collaboration and efficiency towards making the investment time lower with higher productivity by changing the way staff can work together for instruction.

Then, there's the dynamic shift. Students get a more prominent voice than teachers are used to. A whole new power structure instruction now works under, copping the fears uprooted from *Lord of the Flies*. Or, the expectation switches from students getting answers correct to asking the right questions, doing the right research, and finding new ways to come up with a solution.

Project-based learning isn't new, and the concept on its own isn't radically reformist. It's existed for over a century, longer than the system in place, and arguably a better version. The idea on its own isn't radical, but the mainstream pursuit of it is.

Project-based learning makes a big mistake. It vilifies instead of modifies. It appears as a form to prove the other systems wrong. It's a mechanic for pushing change further than how kids are taught. It makes an impression of massive reform when the concept can be built around minor building blocks from its initial components- harnessing natural curiosity. Instead of working towards small building blocks that form active advancement, it harnesses the one percent to outperform. Project-Based learning isn't pure reform inside and out, but how it positions itself is.

In Summary:

- Project-based learning takes a more radical approach towards learning, but the concept on its own has actually existed well before the education system of today. Project-based learning isn't revolutionary, but the method of approach has been.
- Kids being hands-on to learn is a natural strategy that's stood with children since they were babies. It's also a strategy that's been a part of

education since early on; its inception was established in 1907 by discovering an educator named Maria Montessori, who would open up a high-quality daycare center for disadvantaged students. Tactile learning has been both an effective and a standard approach to education that's shown plausible benefit in its implementation.

- Project-Based learning solves the problem of a lack of interaction with course material. It implements an element of play to the learning environment, a change in perspective to execute into learning first and foremost. It starts with a lean approach, even with its broadness.

- In Peter Glenn's piece, "Why Project Based Learning hasn't gone mainstream," Glen explores the more monumental successes of project-based learning, stating that "Some project based schools report 20% higher standardized test scores than those with conventional classrooms". The kids do better- even within the core system already constructed. In fact, it sounds like project-based learning could, in fact, have been the standard, with its effectiveness showing a greater capacity for success before the complete advent of the system, with the grassroots of the education industry already being formed in its own space.

- The reason why it's struggling with implementation is its ask- requiring the need to transform the curriculum, demand better hours of our teachers, and a restructure of the day. But many of these problems have more specific areas where change can be had- such as preparing parents to not be home with their children- allowing for some of the discomforts along longer school days to subside. Or, when it comes to adapting to a new power structure- begin with changing the expectations of the students- not rewire the curriculum.

- Project-based learning is only implemented in 1% of schools nationwide.

Conclusion.

Well, that's a wrap. You've reached the end of this book, and I hope that you found it enjoyable. I also hope that reading this opened your mind to the prospects of a new way to look at how systems change, specifically education.

The point of this book wasn't to make education the enemy or to diminish the success it has brought on. The goal wasn't to tell you why the education industry is terrible or why specific changes absolutely needed to be made. If anything, it was the antithesis of that assumption—that education isn't a political problem that's been static in it's changes, but rather that it already *is* changing. It's just not changing in the way that change first comes to mind- political reform—the type of changes that hits the news, hot off the press.

Instead of being the subject of a reform movement calling for change, education evolves on it's own- from a public credential institution, to more personalized learning experiences, primarily through private experimentation and implementation in the market. People are now being allowed to learn and find the path that befits them. It's not being done through sweeping legislation or fierce attacks towards the dominating policies and institutions today, but by finding tiny problems and fixing them with simple solutions. Solutions that when you look at the extensive list--

- **Clarifying the role of education - Seen in Lambda and Praxis's implementation of** defining themselves in their educating model.

- Honing in on computational thinking over calculation- Seen in Wolfram-Alpha, which focuses on instructing math by acknowledging that computation is automated- opening up the boundaries of how we can teach math.

- Small-step credentials- Seen in Udemy's nanodegree program focused on being able to do specific, small specialties to funnel people into tech jobs as an introductory job.

- Self-focused learning- Allowing the kids to instruct themselves to a greater degree enables teachers to rethink their role in the classroom, focusing on managing and facilitating over pure teaching, as seen in Acton Acadamy.

- Utilizing curiosity to get students to chase the first steps towards mastery- This was seen in Masterclass, which provided a low barrier entry to learning from top-tier experts in their field for people to get started towards learning whatever they wanted

- Making plans for recovering students who might fall behind- This was a key in developing Khan Academy, which emphasized moving forward on a lesson once a topic was mastered first, without pressure.

In many ways, these ideas and changing strategy are akin to the lean-thinking methodology I mentioned throughout the book. The lean-thinking process focuses on solving problems, making the most simple, viable solution around, then utilizing testing and data to create a feedback loop. The strategy is meant to create an upward spiral of change towards startup organizations. Still, as you might have been able to tell with the stories that all gathered in the chapters previous, it's also got a powerful compounding mechanism that can quickly bring change when it's needed.

"The first step is figuring out the problem that needs to be solved and then developing a minimum viable product (MVP) to begin the process of learning as quickly as possible. Once the MVP is established, a startup can work on tuning the engine. This will involve measurement and learning and must include actionable metrics that can demonstrate cause and effect question."

This isn't just about education; it's a survey of what effective reform can look like. It doesn't need to be dominated by loud voices, but small, focused steps that can prove a hypothesis right, attract people towards it, and offer an outlet for solutions when they can't be readily implemented for the masses. Reform isn't about making noise, rebellion, or a coupe-de-ta. It's about change- no matter how big or small, and it starts with mindshifts. It starts with thinking small, asking the right questions to find the correct answers. It is to test, to fail, and to present what works. That's what the core story behind Lambda, Praxis, MasterClass, Udacity, Wolfram-Alpha, Acton Academy, and Khan Academy relies on. It's the component that standards-based grading has found gravel in, and it's the ornament project-based learning that has been missing to make tremendous headway.

Mindshifts proposed a new way to look at change- to look at it in a leaner, more constructive way. If there is anything that education's root has found it's fiercest benefit in, it's change.

I hope you enjoyed the book- and that you picked up a thing or two about lean reform and education. I hope you picked up a mindshift along the way.

Sources

"1981 | Timeline of Computer History | Computer History Museum." 2010. Computerhistory.Org. 2010. https://www.computerhistory.org/timeline/1981/.

Editors, History com. 2017. "Atomic Bomb History." HISTORY. 2017. https://www.history.com/topics/world-war-ii/atomic-bomb-history#:~:text=Robert%20Oppenheimer%2C%20%E2%80%9Cfather%20of%20the.

Espinola, Mark. 2017. "History of the College Grading Scale." GradeHub. 2017. https://gradehub.com/blog/college-grading-scale/#:~:text=The%20first%20college%20grading%20scale.

Goldin, Claudia, and Lawrence F Katz. 1999. "The Shaping of Higher Education: The Formative Years in the United States, 1890 to 1940." Journal of Economic Perspectives 13 (1): 37–62. https://doi.org/10.1257/jep.13.1.37.

"History | Columbia University in the City of New York."
2019. Columbia.Edu. 2019.
https://www.columbia.edu/content/history.

*Hoffman, Chris. n.d. "PCs Before Windows: What Using
MS-DOS Was Actually Like." How-To Geek. Accessed
September 24, 2020. https://www.howtogeek.com/188980/pcs-
before-windows-what-using-ms-dos-was-actually-like/.*
*June 2009, Rich Arzoomanian 26. n.d. "A Complete History
Of Mainframe Computing." Tom's Hardware. Accessed
September 24, 2020.*
*https://www.tomshardware.com/picturestory/508-
mainframe-computer-history.html.*

*"Minimum Wage." n.d. LII / Legal Information Institute.
Cornell.*
*https://www.law.cornell.edu/wex/minimum_wage#:~:text=T
he%20national%20minimum%20wage%20was.*

*Nystedt, Brendan. 2018. "Apple Computers Made for
Schools: EMac, EMate 300, PowerMac G3." WIRED.
March 27, 2018. https://www.wired.com/gallery/how-apples-
education-devices-changed-through-the-years/.*

October 2, Nick Heath in Software on, 2018, and 6:08 Am Pst. n.d. "Inside Windows 10's Ancestor: Five Facts Revealed by MS-DOS' Source Code." TechRepublic. Accessed September 24, 2020. https://www.techrepublic.com/article/inside-windows-10s-ancestor-five-facts-revealed-by-ms-dos-source-code/#:~:text=It%20was%20written%20in%20a.

"Our Documents - Morrill Act (1862)." 2019. Ourdocuments.Gov. 2019. https://www.ourdocuments.gov/doc.php?flash=false&doc=33.

Pollack, Andrew. 1983. "Big I.b.m. Has Done It Again." The New York Times, March 27, 1983, sec. Business. https://www.nytimes.com/1983/03/27/business/big-ibm-has-done-it-again.html.

Tassava, Christopher. 2008. "The American Economy during World War II." Eh.Net. 2008. https://eh.net/encyclopedia/the-american-economy-during-world-war-ii/.

Unger, Robert. 2017. "The Knowledge Economy | Economics Help." Economicshelp.Org. June 26, 2017. https://www.economicshelp.org/blog/27373/concepts/the-knowledge-economy/.

Tozzi, Christopher. 2020. "Mainframe History: How Mainframes Have Changed Over the Years." Precisely. March 4, 2020. https://www.precisely.com/blog/mainframe/mainframe-history.

University, Michigan State. n.d. "Michigan State University - MSU Facts." Michigan State University. https://msu.edu/about/thisismsu/facts.php.

"Where Did The Test Come From? - History Of The Sat - A Timeline | Secrets Of The Sat | FRONTLINE | PBS." n.d. Www.Pbs.Org. Accessed September 24, 2020. https://www.pbs.org/wgbh/pages/frontline/shows/sats/where/timeline.html#:~:text=In%201926%20the%20SAT%20is.

Chapter II Links:

ttps://www.pewsocialtrends.org/2016/10/06/1-changes-in-the-american-workplace/
(https://www.pewsocialtrends.org/2016/10/06/1-changes-in-the-american-workplace/)
https://ourworldindata.org/working-hours
https://discoverpraxis.com/stories/

*https://www.shrm.org/resourcesandtools/hr-topics/compensation/pages/average-starting-salary-for-recent-college-grads.aspx#:~:text=Average%20Starting%20Salary%20for%20Recent%20College%20Grads%20Hovers%20Near%20%2451%2C000,-Starting%20pay%20has&text=Recent%20college%20graduates%20in%20the,Colleges%20and%20Employers%20(NACE).
https://www.insidehighered.com/quicktakes/2020/02/18/41-recent-grads-work-jobs-not-requiring-degree
https://nces.ed.gov/programs/coe/pdf/coe_sbc.pdf*

Sources (Cont.)

ACT. n.d. "Enrollment Management Trends Report | 2012." Accessed October 3, 2020. http://www.act.org/content/dam/act/unsecured/documents/EMTrendsReport2012.pdf.

"ACT FAQs | Testmasters." n.d. Www.Testmasters.Com. Accessed October 3, 2020. https://www.testmasters.com/act/faq#:~:text=information%2C%20click%20here.-.
Clark, Ashley, and Stephen Burd. 2019. "How College Board's Aggressive Campaign to Save the SAT May Kill It." Newamerica.Org. New America. 2019.

https://www.newamerica.org/education-policy/edcentral/how-college-boards-aggressive-campaign-to-save-the-sat-may-kill-it/.

"College Board Search — Student Data by Exam — The College Board." n.d. Collegeboardsearch.Collegeboard.Org. Accessed October 3, 2020. https://collegeboardsearch.collegeboard.org/pastudentsrch/support/about-the-data/student-data-by-exam.

Corp, Harland Clarke Holdings. 2012. "Harland Clarke Holdings Corp. Reports Full Year And Fourth Quarter 2012 Results." Www.Prnewswire.Com. 2012. https://www.prnewswire.com/news-releases/harland-clarke-holdings-corp-reports-full-year-and-fourth-quarter-2012-results-192991431.html#:~:text=Net%20revenues%20for%20the%20Scantron.

"Education: Lobbying, 2020 | OpenSecrets." 2016. Www.Opensecrets.Org. 2016. https://www.opensecrets.org/industries/lobbying.php?cycle=2016&ind=W04.

Figlio, David, and Susanna Loeb. 2011. "School Accountability." In Handbook of the Economics of Education, 383–421. Stanford. https://doi.org/10.1016/b978-0-444-53429-3.00008-9.

"How Do School Funding Formulas Work?" 2017. Urbn.Is. Urban. 2017. https://apps.urban.org/features/funding-formulas/#:~:text=School%20funding%20is%20a%20blend.

"How Much Do the SAT and SAT Subject Tests Cost? - College Board Blog." n.d. Blog.Collegeboard.Org. Accessed October 3, 2020. https://blog.collegeboard.org/how-much-does-sat-and-sat-subject-test-cost#:~:text=For%20the%202019%2D2020%20school.

"NeXt Knowledge Factbook 2010 Knowledge Market Size (2010) Market Size (2013) Growth (CAGR) Market Size (2015) Global Market Size." 2010. https://www.kellogg.northwestern.edu/faculty/jones-ben/htm/NextKnowledgeFactbook2010.pdf.

ProPublica, Mike Tigas, Sisi Wei, Ken Schwencke, Brandon Roberts, Alec Glassford. n.d. "College Board - Nonprofit Explorer." ProPublica. Accessed October 3, 2020. https://projects.propublica.org/nonprofits/organizations/131623965.

"SEDCAR(Standards for Education Data Collection and Reporting)." 1991. https://nces.ed.gov/pubs92/92022.pdf.

Selingo, Jeffrey. 2017. "Colleges Are Tracking Prospective Students' Digital Footprints." The Atlantic. April 11, 2017. https://www.theatlantic.com/education/archive/2017/04/how-colleges-find-their-students/522516/.

*"States That Require the ACT or SAT." 2017. Magoosh Blog |
High School. May 15, 2017.
https://magoosh.com/hs/act/2017/states-that-require-the-act-or-sat/.*

*"The Price of Standardized Testing – Education." n.d.
Sites.Psu.Edu.* https://sites.psu.edu/tota19edu/2019/02/07/the-price-of-standardized-testing/.

*Academy, Khan. 2008. "Khan Academy." Khan Academy. 2008.
https://www.khanacademy.org/about.*

*Beard, Alison. 2014. "Life's Work: An Interview with Salman
Khan." Harvard Business Review. January 1, 2014.
https://hbr.org/2014/01/salman-khan.*

*"Center for American Progress." 2019. Center for American
Progress. Center for American Progress. 2019.
https://www.americanprogress.org/issues/education-
postsecondary/reports/2019/06/12/470893/addressing-1-5-trillion-
federal-student-loan-debt/.*

*Chubb, Chad. 2019. "Student Loans: To Solve the Problem,
Understand the History." Www.Kiplinger.Com. Kiplingers
Personal Finance. June 10, 2019.
https://www.kiplinger.com/article/college/T042-C032-S014-
student-loans-to-solve-problem-understand-history.html.*

Duffin, Erin. 2020. "U.S. College Enrollment Statistics 1965-2027 | Statista." Statista. Statista. March 13, 2020. https://www.statista.com/statistics/183995/us-college-enrollment-and-projections-in-public-and-private-institutions/.
"Federal Financial Aid Policy: Then, Now, and in the Future." n.d. Www.Naspa.Org. Accessed October 5, 2020. https://www.naspa.org/blog/federal-financial-aid-policy-then-now-and-in-the-future#:~:text=Since%201965%20federal%20aid%20to.

"Federal Student Aid." n.d. Studentaid.Gov. https://studentaid.gov/h/understand-aid/how-aid-works.
"InflationData: Education Inflation."n.d. Inflationdata.Com. https://inflationdata.com/inflation/inflation_articles/Education_Inflation.asp.

Allred, Austen. 2017. "Why We Started Lambda School." Medium. November 14, 2017. https://medium.com/lambda-school-blog/why-we-started-lambda-school-cf21a8328bbd.

Gellman, Lindsay. 2018. "Code Now. Pay Tuition Later." The Atlantic. June 30, 2018. https://www.theatlantic.com/education/archive/2018/06/an-alternative-to-student-loan-debt/563093/.

"Lambda School's 2019 Outcomes Report." 2019. Lambdaschool.Com. 2019. https://lambdaschool.com/reports/2019-outcomes-report.

"Praxis | A College Alternative That Leads To A Full-Time Job." n.d. Discoverpraxis.Com. Accessed October 7, 2020. https://discoverpraxis.com/#the-job.

Reini, Josh. 2019. "The Friedman Solution to the Student Loan Crisis | Josh Reini." Fee.Org. September 6, 2019. https://fee.org/articles/isas-the-friedman-solution-to-the-student-loan-crisis/.

Lunden, Ingrid. 2020. "TechCrunch." TechCrunch. 2020. https://techcrunch.com/2020/08/21/lambda-school-raises-74m-for-its-virtual-coding-school-where-you-pay-tuition-only-after-you-get-a-job/.

James, Meg. 2020. "How Disney's Bob Iger Went from Underrated CEO to Hollywood Royalty." Los Angeles Times. March 1, 2020. https://www.latimes.com/entertainment-arts/business/story/2020-03-01/bob-iger-transformed-disney-and-hollywood.

Markovits, Daniel. 2019. "American Universities Must Choose: Do They Want to Be Equal or Elite?" Time. Time. September 12, 2019. https://time.com/5676174/universities-equality-eliteness/.

Newnham, Danielle. 2020. "When You Stop Learning, You're Dead." Medium. February 10, 2020. https://medium.com/swlh/when-you-stop-learning-youre-dead-7976d324b6b7.

Computer-Based Maths: How to Fix Maths Education." n.d. Www.Computerbasedmath.Org. Accessed October 11, 2020. https://www.computerbasedmath.org/.

TED. 2010. "Conrad Wolfram: Teaching Kids Real Math with Computers." YouTube Video. YouTube. https://www.youtube.com/watch?v=60OVlfAUPJg&ab_channel=TED.

Wan, Tony. 2018. "Conrad Wolfram: Let's Build a New Math Curriculum That Assumes Computers Exist - EdSurge News." EdSurge. September 19, 2018. https://www.edsurge.com/news/2018-09-19-conrad-wolfram-let-s-build-a-new-math-curriculum-that-assumes-computers-exist.

"Wolfram|Alpha: Making the World's Knowledge Computable." 2016. Wolframalpha.Com. 2016. https://www.wolframalpha.com/.

Wolfram, Conrad. 2018. "Has the Math(s) Brand Become Toxic?" Conrad Wolfram. 2018. http://www.conradwolfram.com/home/toxicmathsbrand.

Wolpert, Stuart. 2018. "Why so Many U.S. Students Aren't Learning Math." UCLA. UCLA. https://newsroom.ucla.edu/stories/why-so-many-u-s-students-arent-learning-math.

Sources:

"Acton Academy - Schools on EdSurge." n.d. EdSurge. Accessed October 17, 2020. https://www.edsurge.com/schools/acton-academy.

"Acton Academy Placer | Placer County, CA." n.d. Acton Academy Placer. https://www.actonplacer.com/resources.

"Acton Academy Placer | Placer County, CA." ———. n.d. Acton Academy Placer. Accessed October 17, 2020. https://www.actonplacer.com/.
Ark, Tom Vander. n.d. "Acton Academy: Hero Launchpad Goes Global." Forbes. Accessed October 17, 2020. https://www.forbes.com/sites/tomvanderark/2019/08/21/acton-academy-hero-launchpad-goes-global/#5abcb6f6f2fe.

"ELA Standards1." 2012. http://www.corestandards.org/wp-content/uploads/ELA_Standards1.pdf.

"English Language Arts Standards | Common Core State Standards Initiative." 2019. Corestandards.Org. 2019. http://www.corestandards.org/ELA-Literacy/.

Foster, Tom. 2017. "Inside the Schools That Want to Create the Next Mark Zuckerberg--Starting at Age 5." Inc.Com.

February 27, 2017. https://www.inc.com/magazine/201703/tom-foster/kids-inc-entrepreneurship-training.html.
Adams, William, Debra Franklin, Denny Gulick, Frances Gulick, Elizabeth Shearn, Tom Bailey, Davis Jenkins, and Tristan Denley. 2012. "Remediation Is a Broken System. There's a Better Way — Start Many More Students in College Courses with Just-in-Time Support."

https://www.insidehighered.com/sites/default/server_files/files/CCA%20Remediation%20ES%20FINAL.pdf.
Beard, Alison. 2014. "Life's Work: An Interview with Salman Khan." Harvard Business Review. January 1, 2014. https://hbr.org/2014/01/salman-khan.

Horn, Michael B. n.d. "LISTEN — Class Disrupted Podcast Episode 3: Why Can't Sal Khan Just Teach Everyone?" Accessed October 17, 2020. https://www.the74million.org/article/listen-class-disrupted-podcast-episode-3-why-cant-sal-khan-just-teach-everyone/.

*"Project-Based Learning - Khan Lab School." n.d.
Www.Khanlabschool.Org. Accessed October 17, 2020.
https://www.khanlabschool.org/academics/the-kls-model/project-
based-learning.*

*Romero, Esmeralda Fabián. n.d. "How Khan Academy Used a
Successful Experiment With California's Long Beach Unified to
Launch District Partnerships Across the Country." Accessed October
17, 2020. https://www.the74million.org/article/how-khan-
academy-used-a-successful-experiment-with-californias-long-beach-
unified-to-launch-district-partnerships-across-the-country/.*

*"Sal Khan: Test Prep Is 'the Last Thing We Want to Be' - EdSurge
News." 2019. EdSurge. July 16, 2019.
https://www.edsurge.com/news/2019-07-16-sal-khan-test-prep-is-
the-last-thing-we-want-to-be.*

*Washington Post. 2020. "Khan Academy's Sal Khan Shares
Advice for Online Learning: Do Less, and Turn off the Camera,"
August 31, 2020.
https://www.washingtonpost.com/technology/2020/08/31/khan-
academy-remote-learning/.*
*"What Is the History of Khan Academy?" n.d. Khan Academy
Help Center. https://support.khanacademy.org/hc/en-
us/articles/202483180-What-is-the-history-of-Khan-Academy-
#:~:text=How%20was%20Khan%20Academy%20started.*

cidzerda@gazettextra.com, Catherine W. Idzerda. n.d. "Standards-Based Disagreement: Not Everybody Pleased with Grading System." GazetteXtra. https://www.gazettextra.com/news/education/standards-based-disagreement-not-everybody-pleased-with-grading-system/article_a6752bf1-3dcb-5615-8223-b3f451401382.html.

Craig, Theresa. 2011. "Running Head: EFFECTS OF STANDARDS-BASED REPORT CARDS ON LEARNING EFFECTS OF STANDARDS-BASED REPORT CARDS ON STUDENT LEARNING A Thesis Presented By." https://repository.library.northeastern.edu/files/neu:1127/fulltext.pdf.

Davis, Lauren. 2019. "Standards-Based Grading: What to Know in 2019." Schoology.Com. Schoology. February 13, 2019. https://www.schoology.com/blog/standards-based-grading.

"Grades That Show What Students Know - Educational Leadership." 2011. Ascd.Org. 2011. http://www.ascd.org/publications/educational-leadership/nov11/vol69/num03/Grades-That-Show-What-Students-Know.aspx.

Townsley, Matt. 2018. "Better Reflects Knowledge Better Prepared For College/Career Positive Impact On Grades Positive Impact on

School of Choice DATA STANDARDS BASED GRADING SURVEY." https://files.eric.ed.gov/fulltext/ED590391.pdfBG%20Communication.pdf.

Work, Josh. 2014. "3 Peaks and 3 Pits of Standards-Based Grading." Edutopia. George Lucas Educational Foundation. 2014. https://www.edutopia.org/blog/peaks-pits-standards-based-grading-josh-work.

Boss, Suzie. 2011. "Project-Based Learning: A Short History." Edutopia. George Lucas Educational Foundation. September 20, 2011. https://www.edutopia.org/project-based-learning-history.

Glenn, Peter. 2016. "Why Project-Based Learning Hasn't Gone Mainstream (And What We Can Do About It)." EdSurge. EdSurge. April 23, 2016. https://www.edsurge.com/news/2016-04-23-why-project-based-learning-hasn-t-gone-mainstream-and-what-we-can-do-about-it.

Sheehy, Kelsey. 2013. "Tips for Transitioning to Project-Based Learning." US News & World Report. U.S. News & World Report. 2013. https://www.usnews.com/education/blogs/high-school-notes/2013/06/24/tips-for-transitioning-to-project-based-learning.

"Who Was Maria Montessori?" n.d. Amshq.Org. https://amshq.org/About-Montessori/History-of-Montessori/Who-

Was-Maria-
Montessori#:~:text=Maria%20Montessori%20was%20an%20Itali
an.

Chafkin, Max. 2013. "Udacity's Sebastian Thrun, Godfather Of
Free Online Education, Changes Course." Fast Company.
November 14, 2013.
https://www.fastcompany.com/3021473/udacity-sebastian-thrun-
uphill-climb.

Friedman, Jordan. 2016. "What Employers Think of Badges,
Nanodegrees from Online Programs." US News & World Report.
U.S. News & World Report. 2016.
https://www.usnews.com/education/online-education/articles/2016-
01-22/what-employers-think-of-badges-nanodegrees-from-online-
programs.

"Online Tech Courses and Nanodegree Programs | Udacity." n.d.
Www.Udacity.Com. https://www.udacity.com/nanodegree.

"Udacity Nanodegree Reviews: Your Questions Answered." 2015.
Udacity. March 18, 2015.
https://blog.udacity.com/2015/03/udacity-nanodegree-reviews-your-
questions-
answered.html#:~:text=A%20Nanodegree%2C%20provided%20by
%20Udacity.